there is an
answer

there is an answer

EVERETT W. PALMER

ABINGDON PRESS ⟨𝆏⟩ new york • nashville

THERE IS AN ANSWER

Copyright © 1962 by Abingdon Press

Portions of the sermons "Trust in God," "Everybody's Sins," "Walking
on Stilts," "Where Is Security—With Honor?" "What to Do When
Drafted," and "Is Purity Passé?" were first published in Adult Student and
Wesley Quarterly and are copyright 1960, 1961, 1962 by The Methodist
Publishing House. Used by permission.

Library of Congress Catalog Card Number: 62-14668

Scripture quotations unless otherwise noted are from
the Revised Standard Version of the Bible and are copyright
1946 and 1952 by the Division of Christian Education of
the National Council of the Churches of Christ in the U.S.A.

B

SET UP, PRINTED, AND BOUND BY THE
PARTHENON PRESS, AT NASHVILLE,
TENNESSEE, UNITED STATES OF AMERICA

To our daughters
JOANNE, ELIZABETH, and RUTH
each a joy forever

preface

"EVERY HUMAN BEING IS A PROBLEM IN SEARCH OF A SOLU-
tion," [1] Montagu reminds us. No one need venture beyond
himself for confirmation of that observation. Awareness of
problems and search for solutions engage us all from
infancy.

Let no one pity himself. Here is our means of growth,
our way to fulfillment, even the road by which God comes
to us and we to God. This is the great excitement of the
human pilgrimage. Without it ours would be the existence
of fence posts or potatoes.

Problems which arise to dispute the way with us are, of
course, intensely personal. Each comes bearing our own
name and address, often searching and testing us to the
bottom.

But no problem is our monopoly. When we lift our eyes
and look beyond self to others, we find them grappling with
the same adversaries. It is safe to assume no major problem

[1] Ashley Montagu, *On Being Human* (New York: Abelard-Schuman,
Ltd., 1950), p. 12.

we confront in the business of living is altogether a stranger to other men, past or present.

Such human problems, common to us all, are the concern of the chapters which follow. Take the matter of belief or disbelief in God. What reasons do we have for believing in a Christian God? Why should we trust him, especially when trouble and suffering are the wages of virtue?

We hear it said, "Now, have faith." "But," we ask, "how?" Is there a faith that is not make-believe, a denial of reason? Whence comes faith that wins assent of mind and heart; that transforms ordinary men, as the New Testament bears witness, until their deeds are those of giants?

Consider the Bible. Why do so many turn from it in bewilderment and boredom? Why does it give rise to confusion and misgiving? How can it be for us the Book of books: the wisdom, strength, joy, and peace of God for our daily lives; the way of salvation; our dearest treasure? What thoughtful person has not confronted such questions?

Or, we ask, "Why be decent?" Why make the effort for goodness when it seems to be a path that winds forever uphill? What is the use, we wonder, when loneliness, persecution, and pain are our rewards?

There are the problems indigenous to marriage, the lot of husbands and wives the world around; those rising from our yearning for a sense of worth; and those that meet us when trouble comes like a thief in the night. There are those which confront us in the rebellion of youth, in the burden of monotony, in the suffering of the innocent, and in the fact of death.

In the world of frightened men, where many would sell

their souls for a shred of security, we ask: "Where can we find security that is security and worthy of honorable men?"

Where is the citadel of quietness in these tangled and turbulent times where we may find ourselves, be found of God, and gain empowerment for achieving the good we would do?

We call Jesus Christ "Savior." How can he save us?

These are questions arising from problems that engage most, if not all, of us. Their dimensions reach across the whole of life. They involve issues of greatest moment and weigh us in the balances.

As we deal with them we can be helped by the experience of other men, especially those who have come under the influence of Jesus Christ and have discovered his saving power. The wisdom they have won is earth's best gift—and heaven's, too.

This I have discovered. This I share.

Again, may I express appreciation to LaVerne Briscoe, who has given thoughtful and earnest secretarial support; also to Jean Carr, who provided valued assistance. Especially I acknowledge supreme indebtedness to my wife, Florence R. Palmer, without whose encouragement and faith this book could not have been written.

Everett W. Palmer

contents

chapter one

WHY BE DECENT, ANYWAY?

WHY BE DECENT? WHY TRY TO DO THE RIGHT? CIRCUM-stances and requirements for decision drive that question straight at our hearts every day.

In any moral choice evil usually appears easier and more inviting than virtue. Goodness often appears to be a stony path that winds forever uphill.

Why make the effort?

Here is a lad in military service. He is far from home, lonely and bored. Time hangs heavy. He is among strangers. Nobody cares what he does so long as he conforms to military regulations and obeys orders. He has a weekend leave. The fellows he is with set out on a tour of the local bars and brothels. He knows that is wrong; he would never do it at home. But it is hard to think of anything else to do, embarrassing to be ridiculed by your buddies. It is awkward to be left alone in a strange place with no one you know and nothing to do. Why should he be decent?

A woman has married a weakling. He cannot leave liquor alone—and never holds a job. He wanders off for a month—even a year—at a time. There are two small children. She is attractive, intelligent, capable, virtuous. She supports the family and does well at her job. Like any woman in her predicament in a cosmopolitan community, she is subject to strong temptation. She has fought the good fight and won it—all the way to the present. But she is lonely and discouraged. In darker moments she wonders, "Why should I keep on trying?" She thinks of this especially after a long, hard day when she trudges home, weary and footsore, to her meager back apartment. Other women ride by with successful husbands in shiny cars, bound for comfortable homes. Among them are several whose place she could usurp by so much as lifting her little finger. She thinks, "They haven't tried half so hard as I to do what is right. Yet, this is what I get. Why should I keep on trying?" Why should she?

A man is struggling to make his business succeed. He has had bad breaks. Then comes the chance he has been hoping for, a deal that will put him on his feet. At first it looks all right. It is everything he needs. Later he learns some of it must be under the table. He considers what the money will mean to the future of his business at this crucial juncture. He thinks of his family, of his own dreams. Why should he turn it down and risk failure?

Honesty, purity, courage, loyalty, unselfishness, forgiveness—every virtue is a tall fortress on a high hill. Each is hard to attain, difficult to win. Always it is easier to yield to a temptation than to resist and master it. Why make the effort? Why be decent?

What incentives for goodness are available?

Near at hand, of course, are the motives of self-interest.

No doubt the most ancient and prevalent is that of self-protection. Do we want to keep out of trouble, protect ourselves from injury, pain, disgrace, punishment? Very well, then, be good.

We live in a moral universe. There are laws for the governance of human behavior just as there are laws that rule the destiny of planets and potatoes. Violation of moral law gets us into trouble, even as driving in the wrong lane of a freeway brings us into difficulty. We are punished by our sins.

Observe the religious practices of the world's most primitive people. That is their belief. Study the literature of all great civilizations before the Christian Era, whether Egyptian, Babylonian, Persian, Chinese, Indian, or Grecian. That also is their belief. With one accord they declare: "Would you escape punishment both here and hereafter? Be good!"

Throughout the Bible, likewise, we find blunt and terrible warnings against the consequences deriving from violation of moral law. Christianity teaches that no man can do evil and get away with it: "Whatsoever a man soweth, that shall he also reap." (K.J.V.)

This is a moral universe. God expresses an opinion on the behavior of men and of nations. We are punished by our sins, here and hereafter. If you would keep out of trouble, be good! Fear of consequences, self-protection: that is the most primitive motive for goodness. But it has a legitimate and necessary place in our lives.

Another motive for goodness is self-respect. We have an inner desire for decency. As a bird desires a clean nest, so man wants a sense of inner cleanness, self-approval. This is represented in the noblest of Stoic literature, especially in the writings of Seneca and Epictitus. It was the chief motive for goodness among the American Indian. It is dominant in the culture of the Orient, where often men have preferred death to loss of "face."

Also, this motivation for righteousness always has had an honored place among Christians. Paul voiced it repeatedly: "[Be] a workman who has no need to be ashamed"; "Let your . . . life be worthy of the gospel"; "I have fought the good fight, I have finished the race, I have kept the faith." Kagawa, the great Christian of Japan, said the same when he declared: "I say to my soul, let avalanche come! Let hurricanes roar! Let typhoons unite their forces and rage! Let earthquakes rock and rend! I fear none of them." [1]

You have to live with yourself. Conduct yourself so you can enjoy self-respect. That is a motive for goodness.

In addition to desire for self-protection and self-respect is the motive of self-fulfillment. This may be considered the noblest of all pre-Christian incentives for righteousness. Prior to the coming of Christ it was expressed best of all by the Greeks, especially Plato. Refrain from sin, they taught, because it is self-defeating. Only by way of the discipline of virtue, truth, and beauty can man truly satisfy his human hungers, develop his uniquely human powers, and thus enjoy life. Jesus likewise appealed to this incentive. "I am come," he declared in one of the most quoted verses of the Bible, "that they might have life, and that they might have it more abundantly." (K.J.V.)

Why be decent? Why struggle to do the right? Why take the hard, uphill road of virtue? Out of the dim origins of history comes the answer of self-interest. Be good for the reasons of self-protection, self-respect, and self-fulfillment.

[1] William Axling, *Kagawa* (New York: Harper & Brothers, 1932), p. 25.

But self-interest, however enlightened, is never enough. Motives for righteousness rising out of self-interest, though of themselves legitimate and necessary, are not adequate.

Men of the ancient world remained defeated in the ruins of their best efforts, taunted by ideals of excellence before which they were impotent. It is significant that the supreme literary expression of the Greeks, whose civilization was the flower of the ancient world, was tragedy; and that of the noblest Romans, Stoicism.

But Jesus Christ brought a new and mightier motive for goodness to men. Gathering up and cleansing the old self-interest incentives, he added another, the greatest of all —love.

We gain incentive for goodness because of love for God, love rising in response to his love for us.

God is good to us, far beyond our deserts. Who can awaken in the morning with the world at spring, walk out of doors to the music of birds singing the songs of spring, breathe the clean, sweet air of spring, look upon shrubs, trees, and flowers lovely in the garb of spring and not give thanks to God for the privilege of being alive! Who can test his strength against the demands of honest work and the challenge of difficulties; rejoice in the rewards of friendships and the blessings of family life; or have the incomparable treasure of support given by those who love and trust him, despite knowing all his faults—and not lift his heart to God in gratitude! Who can look at the Cross, seeing there love that shares our predicament and tragedy, yet makes possible victory over sin and death, and not have reason to sing:

17

> Since from His bounty I receive
> Such proofs of love divine,
> Had I a thousand hearts to give,
> Lord, they should all be Thine.

That is reason for goodness. We love him because he first loved us. And loving him, we want to please him, obey him, serve him, work with him. "If you love me," said Jesus, "you will keep my commandments."

Love is a stronger motive for goodness than self-interest. It is one thing to be honest because we believe it is the best policy, working out in the end to our best interests. It is quite something else to be honest because we love and are loved and trusted.

Again and again temptation will prove too strong if we have no defense stronger than self-interest. Indeed, temptation always comes in the guise of self-interest. But our defense against evil is impregnable and our armament for righteousness is invincible when built of love, love for one who first loved us and gave himself for us.

Also, we find incentive to do the right not only in our love for God, but also in our love for people, all people as his children, our brothers and sisters in him.

This is sparkling new. It is original with Jesus of Nazareth. We do not find it in other world religions or philosophies. It is not in Plato. The Stoics knew nothing of it. Buddhism comes nearest to it, but misses it in vague generalities.

Of course, this is not to say people of the ancient world did not know the power and the glory of human love. The era before Christ was rich in the tradition of good fellowship, love between friends, husbands and wives, parents and children. All ancient religions taught men to love their families and neighbors.

The uniqueness of Christianity rests in its definition of what love is and of what its function should be. In essence, according to Jesus, it must be applied not only to the family circle and to those we call friends, but to those we have reason to call enemies, too. It means thinking, wishing, praying, and acting in ways that will do them good. This does not mean we should be honey and cream to everyone. Jesus certainly was not. It may mean reproof, even physical punishment. Jesus did that. It does mean our thoughts and actions must always be for their good, not for our revenge.

When goodness is motivated by Christian love toward others, it does not stop to calculate the gain or loss for self. There is a noble and glorious abandon about it. It reminds one of the athlete who forgets himself in the game, ignoring injury.

Everyone who has played football has a favorite story. I have mine. Some time ago, while digging into some old keepsakes, I came upon a picture, faded and tattered, taken of the last football game in which I was a player. It was Thanksgiving Day morning, the final game of the season. A snowstorm had started the night before, and by game time it had become a blizzard. Throughout the game officials called time every fifteen or twenty minutes and snow plows would scoot up and down the field to clear it enough to permit continuance of play. The snowbanks surrounding the field were so high the spectators huddling on the sidelines could little more than see over them. It was snowing so heavily a high punt sent the ball out of sight. Those of us who did the receiving ran in the general direction where its descent might be expected and then stood peering up in the snow, waiting and hoping. Furthermore, it was bitter cold.

In short it was a miserable day, even for football. But strange to say, I cannot recall that we felt the cold or were much bothered by the snow. Once, when we were coming back for the huddle the quarterback, whom we called Swede, remarked before calling the next play, "What do you know! I think I broke my wrist on that last play."

We looked and replied, "No, it's not broken. Besides, it's your left wrist. Forget it, let's go." With but one arm, he was better than anyone we had on the bench. We did not intend to lose him unless dire necessity required it. So, shrugging his shoulders, he called the next play.

He played the entire game and never said another word about his wrist. He called the plays, ran interference like a demon, and took his turn carrying the ball—in short, he played a smashing game, one of the best of his career.

When the game was over and we were back in the locker room, his forearm was swollen so badly we had to cut off his jersey. The team doctor asked, "How long did you play with that broken wrist?" Once again he shrugged, "Oh, it happened in the first quarter. I didn't feel it much."

Forgetting of self is the glory of any great team sport, both for those who play and those who watch. It also is the glory of Christian living.

We don't measure out things for people on a profit or loss basis; we do all the good we can because we love them.

So the glory begins in our heart. And that is the healing of the world.

Before starting a vacation trip by car, first we write for maps or talk with a friend who has made the journey. But something else needs our attention: we must put gas in the tank. Again and again we must stop for replenishment.

Life is a journey for which we have been given excellent maps. Most of us know the way. Our problem is the gas tank. When we wonder, "Why make the struggle for goodness," it is helpful to pause and give thought to our own best interest, to our concern for self-protection, self-respect, and self-fulfillment. More important, that is the occasion to think about God: remembering how much he loves and trusts us, recalling what he expects of us in behalf of our brothers and sisters, his children. Therein is power for the long road and the steep hill.

chapter two

WHERE IS THIS BUS
GOING?

HALFORD LUCCOCK, WHOSE KINDLY WIT STRUCK MANY A spark for us lesser mortals, once told of the man in New Haven who sprinted madly to board a bus. Lunging through the door and up the steps, he staggered red-faced and panting down the aisle, collapsing in the first vacant seat. Finally, when able to speak, he inquired, "Hey, where is this bus going?"

Our generation has several unfortunate characteristics, not least of which is resemblance to the man who ran for the bus. Especially this is recognized as the hallmark of Americans. Those who visit among us from other lands seem appalled at the blatant, feverish, and pointless haste of our living. By comparison, it is said, we make the rest of mankind seem as still as the stars and as quiet as the moon.

A prominent executive is a "man who has arrived." Having his origins in an old-fashioned farm house, reared by godly parents of humble means, he worked his way through a midwest college. A representative of a national firm, visiting the campus during his senior year, offered him a job. So he began at the bottom of the "organization-man" ladder.

From there he has climbed, emerging time and again as foremost—according to his company's yardstick—among his peers. Promotion has followed promotion. Envious eyes have followed his rise. He has reached the summit: penthouse office, plush surroundings, salary in six figures, national reputation, swank home, and a glamorous wife. His career is ballyhooed as the American success story.

But along the way he has lost his way. He is still successful, still the razor-sharp, hard-driving man of genius in the eyes of his associates. But what he knows about himself he does not like. Indeed, it frightens him. He would give it all back, he says, if he could just be the man his father was. "My father was the rich man," he confesses. "That backwoods farmer of whose country ways I once was ashamed—he was the success, not me. I have become a phony, a million-dollar phony! He had integrity. He knew God. He could go to bed at night with an easy conscience and sleep. He had some peace down deep inside. But me— I'm jittery as a monkey on a wire with nowhere to go."

"Where is this bus going?" Who would say he is not in need of the ministry of quietness? "Better is a handful of quietness," once counseled an ancient wise man of Israel, "than two hands full of toil and a striving after wind." (Eccl. 4:6.) That speaks to our condition.

He was not depreciating the importance of action. Rather, he was warning again the folly of chasing madly after buses, destination unknown. Even the most earnest endeavor is to no avail, he was saying, unless blessed again and again with the ministry of quiet contemplation and inner awareness.

Lest every good intention and worthy endeavor be but "a striving after wind," we must stake our claim upon "a handful of quietness."

What transpires in that time and place where we shut the door against the world's loud roar, bid all our strivings cease, and invite our soul to quietness? A mighty commerce with destiny, enterprise that dwarfs all else to the dimensions of tiddlywinks.

Here we meet self face to face. We achieve identity, learn our name. We look upon what we are and know what we are meant to be.

We attempt concealment of our real self from others, hiding under many a mask, fleeing behind walls of pretense. But when we enter into stillness the masquerade ends, each trusted covert fails. We may deceive others, not ourselves.

Self-confrontation may be avoided by immersion in trivia, passionate pursuit of status and security, and generally keeping too busy to think; by slipping down back alleys of illicit sex or taking refuge in a bottle.

But within the citadel of quietness our soul stands inspection. All that is property of the soul is summoned for judgment: every motive, goal, hope, and aspiration. All that is potential within us knocks at the door of our awareness: every dark depth and shining height, all that is "the grandeur and misery of man."

Nothing good could begin for the prodigal son, our Lord

reminds us, until "he came to himself." That observation, we have good reason to believe, includes us.

There is given in "a handful of quietness" that stark encounter, that moment of truth, by which we come to know ourselves.

Here likewise we not only find ourselves but are found of God. As Elijah discovered, God is not in the roaring wind, nor in the earthquake, nor in the fire. Rather, he is in the still, small voice. He is not known in the press and clamor of the crowd. His presence is felt, his voice heard, when the furor of our striving ceases, the babel of our talking abates, and there is stillness.

For a number of years we lived in a delightful small city. Our home was just three blocks from the broad beaches of the Atlantic. By day we scarcely knew the ocean was there, apart, of course, from the tang of sea air. But at night, when cars and buses no longer buzzed by in steady procession, the staccato of women's heels no longer drummed the sidewalks, nor sounds of human voices filled the air; when the streets were still, houses darkened and every man-made noise hushed by slumber—then we knew the ocean was there! Then we could hear the mighty organ of the deep. Its awesome music of unbroken rhythm and insistent beat rolled unhindered up the streets and down the avenues from home to home. Night after night I was sung to sleep by the voice of the deep.

The ocean was there by day and by night, but how little we knew it until we were still. So God is here, "closer than breathing, nearer than hands and feet," yearning to bless with what we need most, waiting only the open door. He is here; the Sovereign of the universe awaits our hospitality, but we know it not until we are willing to be still and listen.

Also, thus we gain empowerment for whatever good we would do.

As Samuel Miller, dean of Harvard Divinity School, reminds us in a most perceptive book, *The Life of the Soul*, there are really two worlds. One is the obvious world in which man puts his hand to the plow, his shoulder to the load, and gets things done. This is the world of human striving and sweat, the world of action. Here we must live much of the time.[1]

But there is another world, never insistent, least obvious, but immensely more important. This is the world beyond our hands, above the reach of our striving; the world of the infinite and eternal, which, to use the words of Immanuel Kant, "fills the mind with ever an increasing wonder and awe." It is the world of the spirit, of art and music, of wisdom and inspiration, of contemplation and prayer, of religion! This is the world man may enter only if he will be still and ready to receive; only if he comes, not to demand, but to obey. Until man becomes a citizen of this world all he does in the world of his striving is futile, often destructive; at best a "striving after wind."

No one knew this better than Jesus Christ. He had just begun his ministry, crowds clamored for him, success was overwhelming. Also, the first grim portents of opposition had appeared. His own townsmen had scorned and rejected him. John the Baptist, his beloved kinsman and forebear, had been murdered by Herod, his head served upon a

---

[1] (New York: Harper & Brothers, 1951), pp. 103, 104.

platter at the whim of a dancing girl. Our Lord was very much a citizen in the world of action. But he was careful to maintain citizenship in the other world. So we read that at day's end, "after he had dismissed the crowds, he went up into the hills by himself to pray. When evening came, he was there alone."

He loved men and labored mightily to serve them, but went apart from them to be alone and still, receptive to God his Father. We picture him a solitary figure on a hilltop at sunset, remaining alone under the stars with face uplifted. We see him staying in a wilderness or kneeling in a garden. We remember how he returned to his task in a busy world of striving men, often striding through the dawn, always renewed, empowered for the good he would do.

When we compare our hectic, feverish little lives with his life, then we know our great need, again and again, for "a handful of quietness." Therein we find ourselves and are found of God. Of this comes adequate empowerment for the good we would undertake.

Granting our need, how can we avail ourselves of such a ministry?

First, and most obvious, it is simply a matter of choice. There is more to do than we can get done, more to buy than we have money to spend, more places to go than we can attend. We live amidst a deluge of appeals and claims upon our time and attention, money and strength. We select what to us is of greatest value and importance.

Certainly we of twentieth-century America should most frequently be able to lay claim upon "a handful of quietness." We need fewer hours for our livelihood, have more gadgets, conveniences, and creature comforts than our grandparents could have imagined in wildest flights of fancy. What do we do with this extra time and energy?

Harry Golden tells of his immigrant mother living in the Lower East Side of New York at the turn of the century. She was a primitive woman, he says, and could speak only Yiddish. In addition to doing all her own housework, she sewed professionally.

My mother kept the sewing machine in the kitchen near the stove. The stove did not start at the turn of a dial. It took kindling and coal, and sometimes when the coalman did not show up she had to go down four flights to get enough to start the supper fire. She cooked, washed, cleaned, sewed, got everybody off to work and to school, was all ready for them when they returned, emptied the drip pan under the icebox, and every afternoon she sat looking out of the window for a couple of hours.[2]

It is he who tells of the occasion when the *New York Times* sent a reporter to interview Mr. Roebuck on his ninetieth birthday. The reporter began with the usual routine, "To what do you attribute your longevity and good health?" The old gentleman cut him short. "Son," he said, "I sold out to Mr. Sears; Mr. Sears made ten million dollars and now he is dead. Mr. Sears sold out to Julius Rosenwald, who made three hundred million dollars and now he's dead. . . . Tell your readers, that on his ninetieth anniversary,

[2] *Only in America* (Cleveland, Ohio: The World Publishing Company, 1958), p. 305. Copyright © 1958, 1957, 1956, 1955, 1954, 1953, 1951, 1949, 1948, 1944 by Harry Golden.

Mr. Roebuck took his usual walk in Central Park." [3]

It is truly a matter of choice. Once we are sensible enough to put first things first, we cultivate citizenship in the world of the spirit, we invite our soul to quietness.

Second, it is derived from the practice of long-tried and proved religious disciplines: reflective and devout reading of the Bible, regular church attendance, family worship, daily private devotions, the observance of one day each week as a holy day, reserved for attendance upon God and nurture of the soul. Any of these practices, each of itself, is an oasis for the soul in the sun-blistered journey of life. Each is rich in reward as "a handful of quietness."

Herman Wouk, distinguished author and playwright, famous for *The Caine Mutiny* and *Marjorie Morningstar*, in a more recent book tells of his return to religion, the faith of his fathers. He relates:

It was my lot to reach quite young what many people consider the dream life of America: success by my own efforts, a stream of dollars to spend, a penthouse in New York, forays to Hollywood, the companionship of pretty women, all before I was twenty-four. . . . There I was in the realms of gold. . . . But even as I lived this conventional smart existence . . . and dreamed the conventional dreams, it all seemed thin.[4]

So, he says, he gathered his courage and took a long leap. He returned to the religion, Orthodox Judaism, in which he had been born. It has resulted in steadily deepening faith

---

[3] *Ibid.*, p. 262.
[4] From: *This Is My God* by Herman Wouk. Copyright © 1959 by the Abe Wouk Foundation, Inc. Reprinted by permission of Doubleday and Company, Inc. P. 273.

and perceptivity, a life rewarding beyond comparison to that of his first success. Telling what observance of an Orthodox Jewish Sabbath from Friday sundown until twilight of Saturday means to him, he says: "Leaving the gloomy theatre, the littered coffee cups, the jumbled scarred-up scripts, the haggard actors, the shouting stage-hands, the bedevilled director, the knuckle-gnawing producer, the clattering typewriter, and the dense tobacco smoke and backstage dust, I have come home. It has been a startling change, very like a brief return from the wars." Then he describes their custom of family worhip. Saturday, he says, is healing for the whole week. "It is an oasis of quiet," which renews and prepares him for his best work. Once on return, he reports, his producer said to him: "I don't envy you your religion, but I envy you your Sabbath." [5]

For what "a handful of quietness" can give our needy hearts, let us be sensible enough to profit by wisdom of the ages and practice the long-proved disciplines of religion.

Third, be alert to enter unexpected openings for the soul into quietness and communion with God. Use special opportunities. Always we may find some door opening into an oasis.

There are the few minutes we must spend waiting for a bus on some crowded corner. Instead of chafing or sitting numb like potatoes, we can invite God's presence, and in those moments walk with him into green pastures, beside still waters.

Or, there is that moment at night when, after the garage

[5] *Ibid.*, pp. 59, 60.

door has been closed, we stand under the stars. Instead of trudging into our respective houses like drones, we can look up and let the winds of heaven sweep pettiness out of our souls.

Walter Rauschenbusch tells of his adventure:

In the castle of my soul
Is a little postern gate,
Whereat, when I enter,
I am in the presence of God.
In a moment, in the turning of a thought,
I am where God is,
This is a fact.

When I enter into God,
All life has meaning,
Without asking I know;
My desires are even now fulfilled,
My fever is gone
In the great quiet of God.
My troubles are but pebbles on the road,
My joys are like the everlasting hills.

The world of men is full of jangling noises.
God is a great silence.
But that silence is a melody
Sweet as the contentment of love,
Thrilling as a touch of flame.[6]

Available to each of us in the mercy and wisdom of God is "a handful of quietness." Treasure incomparable, it awaits only the seeking heart.

[6] Walter Rauschenbusch, "The Postern Gate." Used by permission of Carl Rauschenbusch.

chapter three

EVERYBODY'S SINS

SIN IS EVERYBODY'S PROBLEM. WE QUICKLY RECOGNIZE IT as Russia's problem, as our neighbor's, or our boss's. But it is our problem, too—a matter strictly personal. "If we say we have no sin," writes the author of I John, "we deceive ourselves, and the truth is not in us."

Sam Jones, famous evangelist of the past generation, was accustomed to challenging large congregations which assembled to hear him with the question: "Does anyone know or has anyone heard of a perfect man?" Always a long silence followed as Brother Sam searched the hall with piercing eyes. Never did anyone rise to answer.

This went on for years. Then one night a man in the rear stood and shouted, "Yes!" Everyone was astonished— no one more than Sam Jones.

Do you mean to say you know or have heard of a perfect man?" queried Sam Jones. "Yes sir!" the man replied. "I don't know him, but I sure have heard of him. He was my wife's first husband."

Only in a Shangri-La of carefully winnowed and seasoned memories can such a creature be found. Sin is everyone's problem. That includes you and me.

Furthermore, sin is our most serious problem. Sin is sickness of the soul which, if unchecked, brings death. God's purpose for us is health and well-being of body and spirit. "I came," said Jesus, "that they may have life and have it abundantly." Sin is the self-centeredness and self-worship which refuses co-operation with that purpose. Sin is the deification and indulgence of self. That is the way, not of life abundant, but of sickness, misery, and death.

"The most terrible consequence of sin," observes Harrison Franklin Rall,

is sin itself. The casual sin becomes the habit and character of the man. Men receive what they desire. They make self the center, and selfishness, with its isolation and emptiness and loneliness, becomes their lot. They refuse God, and theirs is a life without high purpose or hope, without strength and joy and peace. They choose darkness rather than light, and the light that is in them becomes darkness. In the conflict within they let the lower self have its way until at last there is no other." [1]

Paul was on target when he said, "The wages of sin is death." This is death which in measure of consequence makes physical death a triviality scarcely deserving mention. For the death which sin works is the destroyer of the inner man, of all we are meant to become as children of God, and from time into eternity.

Is there an answer to the problem? a physician for this most fatal of all human sickness? Is there a remedy? Yes! We have "good news"! "If we confess our sins, he [God] is faithful and just to forgive us our sins, and to cleanse us

---

[1] *Religion as Salvation* (Nashville: Abingdon Press, 1953), p. 78.

from all unrighteousness." (K.J.V.) In the grace of God we can win a victory over sin. The New Testament and Christian experience through the generations since offer a laboratory record. While the victory is of God, certain action is required of us.

Victory over sin begins with remorse for sin. So long as we are content with sin it has complete power over us. We are its creature. A student will cheat so long as he is content with cheating. An employee will steal from his employer so long as he is content with stealing. A person will be vindictive so long as he is content with hate.

We become content with sin for a curious reason. Sin has what might be described as a hypnotic effect. The more we are in the grip of a particular sin, the more we are detached from reality concerning its nature; the more we regard it not as evil, but as virtue!

For example, the student who habitually cheats soon ceases to view cheating as evil. It becomes to him merely a technique for getting along in the world, like learning how to drive a car or to make a Windsor knot in his necktie. The successful thief has long since ceased to have qualms of conscience about stealing. It has become for him an attainment, an art if you please. He takes pride in it. The big-time racketeer suffers no sleepless nights in sympathy for his victims. Prostitution, dope, and graft have become for him a business, like making furniture or selling potatoes. The person who habitually vents his feelings of frustration and hostility upon others by pouncing upon them with a whiplash tongue does not think of himself as cruel. He takes secret pride in his facility for telling people off. He believes himself virtuous in thus speaking his mind.

Sin always is attempting to brainwash us into believing it is virtue, not sin. The longer we are in a sin's grip, the more success it has in thus deceiving us. This is brainwashing which works the ultimate betrayal.

Something must happen that will break the spell of evil over us. Something must open our eyes to what is truth and beauty and goodness until we recognize and loathe the evil that has enthralled us. This experience of illumination occurs when we bring ourselves into the presence of whatever is true, good, and beautiful. It comes through the ministry of great music and great literature; through association with noble people and through the inspiration of worthy teachers; through thoughtful reading of the Bible and through prayer; in the experience of worship and meditation; in the quietness of a starlit night or in the eyes of a small child looking up in trust and love; and, supremely, in remembrance of Jesus Christ and the meaning of the Cross.

When suddenly we see our sin for what it is and know shame for having been its creature, let us thank God. That can be the beginning of our victory over it.

Victory over sin begins with remorse. But remorse must lead to confession. We are inclined to hide our sense of guilt, to put it out of mind, bury it from sight.

Nothing can work greater harm. A sense of guilt buried in the subconscious festers and spreads infection through our whole being, body and soul. What a host of mental ills and of physical ailments with their accompanying misery may be traced to a festering sense of guilt! For this, surgery and medication of various sorts afford merely the temporary relief of a counterirritant.

The story is told of the country bumpkin who, a genera-

tion ago, spent the night in a hotel for the first time.
Having made ready for bed, he attempted to blow out the
electric light as he did the lantern back on the farm. He
had to learn to find and flick the switch before the light
would go off. For the illness and vague distemper born of
guilt, the ministrations of doctors, nurses, hospitals, and
antibiotics is merely a blowing on the light bulb. It is confession which finds and flicks the switch.

To whom should we confess our sin? Always to God.
Before him we should open our heart and pour out the
poison, making sure we hold back nothing. If Roman
Catholic, we would do this through a priest. If Protestant,
believing every man is his own priest, we would confess
directly to God. Often, however, a sense of guilt makes us
feel so lost and apart from God we may need to voice our
confession through the ears of a minister.

Should we confess to any other human being? Sometimes, but not always. One safe rule to follow is: never confess to another what may cause him injury and pain. When
in doubt, limit your confession to God or through a priest
or minister to God.

But when aware of guilt, confess the sin and be rid of
its poison. As Joshua Liebman once pointed out, seal up
a teakettle and place it over a flame, and it will wreck the
house. But let its powerful vapors escape, and the kettle
sings!

Victory over sin requires the release of confession.

Confession must lead to repentance. We should never
linger with confession, nor return to it. We must turn
about, face in the right direction, and start going that way.
We must commit ourselves to God and, in grateful ac-

ceptance of his forgiveness, begin doing the good we once refused.

The prodigal son not only had remorse for his folly and made confession of it; he repented by returning to his father's house with a pledge of obedience. He made a new beginning as a son in his father's house.

Thank God there can be a new beginning. I often recall the poignant lines by Louisa Fletcher Tarkington:

> I wish that there were some wonderful place
>   Called the Land of Beginning Again,
> Where all our mistakes and all our heartaches
>   And all of our poor selfish grief
> Could be dropped like a shabby old coat at the door,
> And never be put on again.[2]

In the grace of God there can be "a wonderful place, called the Land of Beginning Again."

No one need be a prisoner of his past. No person need be forever bound and shackled by previous follies and sins. For every person, in the mercy and power of God as we know him in Jesus Christ, there can be a "second chance," a new beginning, a "land of beginning again." It is ours when in repentance we accept God's forgiveness; when in his strength we face in the right direction and start going that way.

But victory over sin available to us in God's grace is not complete without restitution. True, we can never undo an evil deed, unsay an evil word, unthink an evil thought. Once done, it cannot be undone. But we can, God helping, make amends.

[2] "The Land of Beginning Again."

Here we gain one of the mightiest motives for goodness. The labors of Paul in the service of Christ are beyond compare. No one man has done so much. The magnitude of his achievement, the depth of his devotion, the flame of his zeal always hold me in awe. What was the secret? His experience of Christ as a living presence, yes. But more, Paul remembered standing outside Jerusalem with the crowd that stoned Stephen to death. He remembered when he had hunted down Christians and turned them over to the authorities for imprisonment and death. When Saul, the persecutor of Christians, became Paul, the Christian, he could not bring Stephen back to life nor undo the hurt he had done other Christians. But he could make amends. And this he did in a record of achievement unsurpassed.

Let past wrongdoing be incentive for present "right-doing." Let God help in making amends. That is a Christian's victory of sin.

To make restitution is one of the mightiest motives for goodness, and it brings a healing peace, healing that reaches down to the deepest hurt sin has wrought, injury done our self-respect and sense of integrity.

In *The Nun's Story* Katherine Hulme tells of the saintly priest spending his life serving in a leper colony of the Belgian Congo. A Christlike soul of giant courage and amazing serenity, he was held in awe and affection by all who knew him, pagan or Christian. Only a very few knew his secret. Once when he was a young priest, in a time of weakness, he had betrayed his vows. Service in the leper colony was for him a means of restitution. To be able to give that ministry gave him great peace. It was to him a gift of

God that reached deeply to heal the hurt his betrayal had
wrought in him. So Paul found comfort in making such
amends as he could for the wrong he had done. So may we.
It will heal the heart sin has hurt as will nothing else. This,
too, is a Christian's victory over sin.

chapter four

WHERE IS SECURITY
—WITH HONOR?

"GOD IS OUR REFUGE AND STRENGTH, A VERY PRESENT HELP IN
trouble.

Therefore will not we fear, though the earth be removed, and
though the mountains be carried into the midst of the sea;

Though the waters thereof roar and be troubled, though the
mountains shake with the swelling thereof."

—Ps. 46:1-3 (K.J.V.)

"The Lord of hosts is with us; the God of Jacob is our refuge."

—Ps. 46:11 (K.J.V.)

The man who wrote those words knew the kind of world
we know. Who he was, when and where he lived, we cannot
say with certainty. He was a Jew, of course, sharing the
plight and the promise which have been the anguish and
the glory of Jews through the millenia; a man of sensitive
and valiant spirit who could look the worst full in the face,
yet go forward holding high the banners of hope and faith.
Did he live in the eighth century B.C. when tiny Judah
quaked and bled under a fearsome invasion of the hordes
of Sennacherib? Was the forty-sixth psalm inspired by
Jerusalem's deliverance from that scourge? Or did he live
during the third century when fighting between successors

of Alexander the Great churned that part of the world into bloody tumult? Was the forty-sixth psalm born of those earthshaking days? The scholars are not sure, though probably one or the other is correct.

This much is certain, however: the writer knew what it meant to live in a world shaken and riven by invading armies, burning cities, toppling kingdoms, and conflicting ideologies; a world where respected restraints have been repudiated, trusted landmarks battered down, and old securities lost. He knew what it meant to live in a world where frightened people will sell their souls for even a shred of security. In short, he knew how it feels to live in such a world as that of this twentieth century.

Also, and more important, he knew where and how to find security in such a world—security that is security. He knew where could be had security that is worthy of those who care for freedom, truth, justice, and honor; security which makes for strength not stagnation, courage not cowardice, advance and adventure not retreat. He knew where we could find security—with honor. This is his great contribution for us.

We should recognize at the outset that our search for security, though of itself natural and good, brings us into great danger.

No one should despise his instinct for security. It is as essential to the business of living as hunger for food or the desire to love and be loved. A wise Providence has impregnated our whole being with it, made it a craving deeper than thought, older than mind. Civilization itself is in part the fruit of man's search for security. For this reason we have moved from caves to houses—and now are thinking of moving back into caves. For this reason we have progressed from the hocus-pocus of witch doctors to the miraculous ministry of modern medicine. For this reason we have established such wise and humane practices as life insurance and health insurance, social security and other pensions, safety and health laws for industry, pure food and drug laws, even the use of radar equipment to slow down our horsepower. For this reason we have founded such institutions of sanity and hope as the Red Cross and the United Nations. For this reason we pledge ourselves in marriage until death us do part, establish homes, build churches, and kneel to pray. So a deeply implanted instinct for security serves our good.

But having said that we should quickly recognize it to be dangerous too. Like the power within the atom, it can serve us or destroy us. The search for security brings us into a double peril.

First is the danger of deception, the peril of placing our trust in false security. We can be like the foolish man Jesus once described, "who built his house upon the sand; and the rain fell, and the floods came, and the winds blew and beat against that house, and it fell; and great was the fall of it."

Some have coveted success, believing it would yield security. They have strained and struggled, pushed and elbowed their way toward what for them spelled success. For it they have bartered friends, home, family, marriage, health, even their souls. They have made success their god, worshiped at its shrine, offered up themselves and all things dear as a sacrifice on its altars. Should fortune smile and they win success beyond their dreams—what then? Do they have security? Ask such a person. No, you need not ask. Look into his face!

Success, Aldous Huxley reminds us, using a phrase of William James, is a "bitch-goddess" demanding strange sacrifices of those who worship her.

Some have resorted to cunning, hoping thereby to find security. They have planned and schemed for personal gain at the expense of their fellows. They have exploited human weakness. When others have been stripped of defenses by adverse circumstance, they have pressed for their own advantage without mercy. They have made a sword of their wits and thus sought security. What have they gained?

California has known its share of cunning men. Of them all, none surpassed Collis P. Huntington. In 1850 he was in Sacramento selling merchandise to gold-crazed men, gouging them for every penny the market would bear. With three other Sacramento merchants, Charles Crocker, Mark Hopkins, and Leland Stanford, he created and led a combine which built the Central Pacific and Southern Pacific railroads, and ruled both California and Nevada with an iron hand for a generation.

Irving Stone, in his splendid history of the west, Men to Match My Mountains, tells of Huntington sitting in his little twelve by twelve office in New York City, buying state legislators, congressmen, senators—even judges—as calmly as he bought locomotives and rails. Every man had his price, he believed, and when necessary to buy him that was merely another item in the cost of production. He believed only fools and weaklings gave to charity, or to community causes for the bettering of anything or anybody. When Hubert

H. Bancroft sent a writer to get his life story, all Huntington
could remember for the benefit of posterity were stories
about how he had got the better of other men in various
business deals. The library and art gallery in San Marino
which bears his name was never of his desire or dreams. A
nephew who inherited some of his untold millions turned
that trick on him.[1]

For all his cunning, did he find security? To the end
he was haunted and driven by fears, consumed by fever for
power and more power to keep the power he had.

Everywhere we look there are the toppled houses of those
who built upon sand. In search for security, let us beware
the danger of deception, the peril of placing ultimate trust
in a false security.

And the second peril? It is the danger of paying more
for security than it is worth. We can care too much for
security. It is important to remember that security is not
man's highest good.

For a bag of gold, a sack of potatoes, or a fence post—
yes. For such things security is of supreme importance. But
for man—never! For him security should be secondary.
Much else is more important—such concerns of the soul
as freedom, truth, honor, and godliness. When we seek
security rather than serve such claims of the soul, we sell
our birthright for a mess of pottage. Then we barter
character for comfort, freedom for safety, honor for convenience, godliness for ease. We sell our souls for thirty
pieces of silver.

The instinct for security has educed much of what we

[1] (Garden City, N. Y.: Doubleday & Co., 1956), pp. 294-96, 376-79,
385.

44

term civilization, of course. It serves our good. The fact remains, however, that man becomes truly man and the interests of civilization are best served only as he curbs his instinct for security even as he must curb every other instinct—in obedience to the higher claims of his soul.

Also, it is a fact that in such renunciation of security civilization has its growing edge. Moses turned from the security of Pharaoh's palace and the inheritance of a prince in Egypt to choose a wilderness and the cause of slaves, and his greatness began, even more—a nation began! Roger Williams turned from the security of conforming to ignorance and bigotry, chose a wilderness in midwinter, and his greatness began, even more—a new era in religious freedom for America and all mankind began! Jesus Christ turned from the security of a carpenter shop in a quiet village to choose a wilderness that led to a cross, and his greatness began, even more—God's supreme and saving work of love for the world began!

Security is not man's highest good. Some things are more important.

Our search for security, of itself natural and good, brings us into great peril, a dual danger. One is the danger of deception, the peril of placing our trust in false security. But worse is the peril of paying more for security than it is worth.

Turn now to the discovery proclaimed in the forty-sixth psalm. Where is our security? Where is security with honor? We find it, says the psalmist, in God; through faith in and obedience to the sovereign of the universe.

Here is security in which we can trust. Nature sometimes

turns traitor; there are floods and drought, tornadoes and earthquakes. People sometimes turn traitor; the worst anguish on earth comes of man's inhumanity to man. Nothing of earth can be trusted, admits the psalmist. But God never turns traitor. He can be depended upon, no matter what. "God is our refuge and strength, a very present help in trouble. Therefore will not we fear, though the earth be removed." (K.J.V.)

In this confidence Jesus Christ faced and mastered the worst. We see him in the picture the world can never forget, sitting at a table with his few remaining friends, eating what he knew would be his last supper with them. It was the darkest night of his life. The powers of evil seemed to be winning the battle. All he had so nobly taught and lived was being scorned and repudiated, killed by ignorance, buried under bitterness. He had sought no gain but the good of others, giving himself in love for the least and the last of men. But for this he was hated and plotted against. He loved his country and served its highest good as none other, but he was called a traitor. He loved God and sought to do his will as none other, yet he was accused of blasphemy. People he had trusted and served in kindness had turned against him, friends had deserted him, even the few which remained were uncertain and fearful. Yet in that hour, with the sky caving in, the earth beneath him falling away, and all the might of an evil world smashing in upon him, he remained steadfast. He stood in quiet dignity and spoke words whose moral grandeur and sheer courage have never been surpassed.

Anchored in the one security man can depend upon no matter what, he comforted his friends and sought to strengthen their hands in God. "God loves you," he assured them, "believe in God; serve him, not the selfish ambitions and fears of your own hearts." So he invited them to face the worst with him. "In the world you have tribulation; but be of good cheer, I have overcome the world." He was ready for anything. Nothing could conquer him. Nothing *did* conquer him. And when his friends remembered and obeyed what he told them that night, they were ready for anything. Nothing could conquer them; nothing did conquer them.

Even so, when we remember and obey what he told them and us that night, we too are ready for anything. Nothing can conquer us. God is our refuge and strength. Here is security which can be trusted.

What is more, here is security with honor. When we ground ourselves in the security that comes of faith in and obedience to God, we make no coward's bargain with life. We are delivered from the fatal allurements of false security by dependence upon a higher Security. We are redeemed in a security which makes for strength, not weakness; courage, not cowardice; advance and adventure, not retreat.

Confident that the Lord of hosts is with us, we challenge error and champion truth; we struggle up the steep, hard slopes of moral excellence; we storm the walls of evil; we risk all for the right; we swing open doors to the future that ought to be.

So in the grace of God the earth is lifted from darkness to light and the heart finds its song and its peace.

This is the victory that overcomes the world, even our faith—even for us!

chapter five

TO STAY MARRIED
—AND LIKE IT!

"LOVE AND MARRIAGE," WE HAVE BEEN FREQUENTLY TOLD, "go together like a horse and carriage." How do we keep them together? That is the question.

A young couple rapturously in love and newly married visited an older friend, a trusted counselor. They talked of marriage and asked, "What makes the great difference in marriages? We want to do more than just stay married. We want to stay married and like it. We see some middle-aged people married twenty-five years and longer for whom marriage seems to be a 'thing of beauty and a joy forever.' There are others for whom all the joy and richness of human companionship, to say nothing of love, has long since vanished. They plod along, chained together by vows and circumstance, expecting no glad surprise, resigned to the worst. While their integrity and sense of honor must be admired, where and how did they lose the song and the glory that marriage surely is meant to be?"

In the play *Christopher Blake* Moss Hart deals with the problem of modern marriage and divorce. In the last scene the judge talks with the twelve-year-old son whose world has been shattered by the separation and divorce of his father and mother. The judge, thoughtfully and kindly attempting to re-establish some ground of respect and emotional security for the lad, says: "Chris, the toughest thing in the world that I know of is the relationship between a man and a woman. I tell you, Chris, it's a tribute to the downright courage and decency of men and women that so many do stick it out." [1]

Of course, "sticking it out" is important. Permanence in marriage is a basic essential. When our Lord said, "What therefore God has joined together, let no man put asunder," he voiced the wisdom of the race. When the church asks those who marry to pledge themselves each to the other "till death us do part," it bespeaks our common conviction. Now and again we hear a rebellious voice, but it quickly fades into silence amidst almost universal belief that those who wed should play the game for keeps.

This we believe is a requirement rooted in the nature of love. That depth of devotion which man and woman may have for each other known as "love" is not a fragile flower which blooms merely in fair weather, but a stalwart oak which remains indomitable regardless of the winter gales. It is a man and woman facing the future hand in hand, saying, "We do not know what awaits us yonder. But whatever comes, for good or ill, from here on we shall meet it together: 'For better, for worse, for richer, for poorer, in sickness and in health, to love and to cherish, till death us do part.'"

Furthermore, permanence in marriage we believe is basic for the maintenance of society. Every major institution of

[1] Copyright 1946 by Random House, Inc.

a civilized society, especially a democratic society, requires the foundation of stable home and family life provided by permanence in marriage. By common consent we regard as indispensable the constancy of "till death us do part."

All this is true and good, but it begs the question. It does not deal with the basic matter that concerned the newly-weds and that concerns every husband and wife. Obviously, permanence in marriage is not enough. Of itself it can be boredom insufferable, calamity indescribable, captivity intolerable. It can be the worst dungeon, even hell's outpost, making the face of death a welcome sight. To this fact there have been and are many witnesses. And what of marriages which escape so dire an extremity but merely drift wearily to and from across a drab wasteland of dreary mediocrity and abandoned hopes? Though maintained in permanence, they, too, desecrate the meaning of marriage.

So we face the query, how can love and marriage be kept in the same carriage? How can people stay married—and like it?

Six commandments for marriage will help.

One is this: Thou shalt pay for it, gladly!

This is more than the first and great commandment for all fathers of marriageable daughters. It is a requirement for every bride and groom, the essence of the marriage vows. Listen: "I, John, take thee, Mary, to be my wedded wife, to have and to hold, from this day forward, for better, for worse, for richer, for poorer, in sickness and in health, to love and to cherish, till death us do part, according to God's holy ordinance; and thereto I plight thee my troth." That is but another way of saying, "I accept in love the obligations of marriage. I put my life in pledge for their payment."

Marriage comes at a high price. Indeed, when we think in terms of its fullest sense, including responsibilities of parenthood, what on this earth expects more of us? demands more from us?

Marriage worthy of the name will not be found in bargain basements. Those who shop for it there come forth with shabby merchandise which quickly becomes a disappointment to them and a blight upon the community.

Marriage is expensive, yes. Mightily so. But what, short of heaven, brings richer blessing? What outside the relationship between man and God can yield so great a gladness, so deep a peace, so satisfying a fulfillment? It is ordained of God to be the natural, beautiful, and joyous unfolding of what we were born to become and attain; even as are rose blossoms for their squat, thorny bush.

A good marriage is cheap at any price. It is worth our best. What blind and stupid misers we are when we begrudge its claims, complain at its price, shirk its demands!

Second: Thou shalt learn to be content.

"Content is the Philosopher's Stone," observed Benjamin Franklin, "that turns all it touches into gold." Without it marriage soon becomes an endurance contest.

Paul has a wise and saving word for all husbands and wives. "I have learned," he said, "in whatever state I am, to be content." What Paul learned the grace of God could give him on his difficult and perilous missions is no less available to those who journey forth in matrimony.

Contentment is determined more by outlook than cir-

51

cumstance. Fundamentally, it is the fruit of our thoughts. As Milton said:

> The mind is its own place, and in itself
> Can make a heaven of hell, a hell of heaven.

As a husband and wife think, so shall be the measure of their content.

It would be pleasant for any man to be wed to a woman who has beauty rivaling the charms of a Miss America, the disposition of a Francis of Assisi, the solicitous concern of a Florence Nightingale, and the genius for cooking of a French chef. But even if heaven's gates were left ajar and such a paragon of feminine perfection tumbled forth and were given him to wed, he soon could have a thousand reasons for discontent.

What of those dimensions of masculine perfection which must haunt the dreams of long-suffering wives? Being but a man I cannot conjure them up. But this I know: should everything of which they dream suddenly by miracle be given them, soon they, too, could be miserable with discontent.

Contentment in marriage does not wait upon perfection or anything resembling it, whether in person or circumstance. A million dollars cannot buy it, a Cadillac cannot convey it, Miss America cannot deliver it, health cannot insure it, even living in Utopia cannot promise it.

Rather, contentment is fashioned of potential which, in the mercy and justice of God, everyone shares alike. It is discovered by those who will have eyes to see virtues to praise rather than faults to condemn. It is found by those who will count their blessings rather than tally cause for complaint. It is gained by those who choose to think the brave and beautiful thoughts of faith, hope, and love. Contentment in marriage is made of our own content. Basically it is the fruit of our mind, the harvest of our soul.

Without it marriage with anyone—anywhere—soon becomes a journey into misery. With it there is magic that turns all things common into gold.

Another imperative is: Thou shalt keep on growing.

We say, "They married and settled down." In so far as this speaks for evidence of maturity—steadiness of purpose, emotional stability, self-discipline, concern for the needs and rights of others—we can rejoice. But as we know full well, there is another kind of "settling down." That is surrender to mental sloth, neglect of those disciplines which keep clean and shining the windows of our mind. How easily we become drones, captives of trivia; deaf, dumb, and blind in a world of great books, great music, great beauty, great thoughts. And becoming drones, the emptiness of our lives becomes a smothering burden to ourselves and an affliction to others.

The story is told of a talkative woman whose husband had fled. Apprehended on charges of desertion, he faced the judge.

"Why did you leave her?" asked the man on the bench.

"She talks, talks, all the time talks. She talks by day, she talks by night."

"Well, what does she talk about?"

"She don't say."

And what of the husband whose teen-age son says of him,

"All Pop does when he comes home is look at the paper, turn on the television to a ball game, and get a can of beer. And then he just sits and snores."

What more need be said? To stay married—and like it: Thou shalt keep on growing!

Also, this is essential: Thou shalt be honest.

There is little need to argue for the honesty of "Thou shalt not commit adultery." That goes without saying. It is fundamental to mutual trust and respect essential to marriage. Anything less is a cheapness and betrayal unworthy the name of love.

This is only a starting point for fidelity in marriage. What of the woman who gives promise in the time of courtship that she will be an affectionate, happy wife but who, once she wears a wedding ring, takes on characteristics of a post— even a porcupine? What of the man who in courtship was gentleness, thoughtfulness, and courtesy personified but in marriage quickly becomes harsh, rude, and careless, even cruel? There is the honesty of keeping faith with promises made in courtship. Those who shirk that requirement are thieves in the treasury of marriage.

Lack of integrity is a foe of harmony and happiness for all concerned in any relationship, especially in marriage.

There is also this indispensable commandment: Thou shalt learn to love.

There is more to love than songwriters tell us, more than Hollywood can teach us. There is more to love than we can know on our wedding day, wonderful and thrilling though that love may be.

That love is not enough to last the years; not enough to give marriage the undergirding, sky room, and resilience required. It is not enough to educe and release in a man and woman the qualities required by marriage.

There must be more to love or no one could long stay married—and like it. Evidence of this is everywhere, nowhere more so than in Hollywood.

What is needed we see in the face of Jesus Christ, the kind of love Paul described when he wrote:

Charity suffereth long, and is kind; charity envieth not; charity vaunteth not itself, is not puffed up, doth not behave itself unseemly, seeketh not her own, is not easily provoked, thinketh no evil; rejoiceth not in iniquity, but rejoiceth in the truth; beareth all things, believeth all things, hopeth all things, endureth all things.   —I Cor. 13:4-7 (K.J.V.)

This is love for which all else is prelude. It is too big, of course, for our small hearts to encompass, but it fills them always to overflowing and stretches them ever larger. It is too vast for our little minds to comprehend entire, but that which they grasp is noblest wisdom.

This is love which makes the years of marriage bring an ever-increasing largess of strength, joy, and peace.

Supremely: Thou shalt share dedication to the highest.

Nicolai Berdyaev has said, "Nothing is so terrible as a man with nothing above him." If that is true for man in the singular, it is no less true for him in the plural.

Marriage needs what can lift it above the level of self-interest, above the crassness of mutual arrangement by which each may exploit the other, or above the shallow futilities of secular living.

Marriage requires the windows and the horizons of great religion. It demands the upward and outward pull of that which is above and beyond us. It needs the challenge and compulsion for growth which comes of dedication to that which deserves and commands our best. It decrees the discipline and dignity of sanctions higher than personal whim or desire. It must have the transforming and ever-renewing spiritual power which enters man through worship and the yielding of his will to God. In short, marriage needs Christ and the church.

What every marriage demands, Christ and the church can and must provide. To stay married—and like it!—thou shalt share dedication to the Highest.

chapter six

WALKING ON STILTS

EVERYONE WANTS A SENSE OF SIGNIFICANCE, A FEELING OF importance. This is as necessary to our well-being as food and water.

The late John P. Marquand, distinguished novelist, told in a magazine article of his visit to a remote tribe in East Africa. He reported attending, during the course of his stay, a sacrificial and ceremonial "rain" dance. Approximately five hundred tribesmen, together with their wives and children, attired in little more than jewelry about their necks and ankles, assembled to participate. More amazing than the spectacular lack of attire among the participants, he wrote, was the costume of the two enormous chiefs who presided. Each was decked out with a felt hat surmounted by an ostrich plume, a white shirt, and a tie. The tie of one apparently had been given by an American on Safari. It showed a nude girl in a cocktail glass bearing the assuring slogan, "Good Health." This neckwear he considered the ultimate as a sign of status indicative of his rank. By means of that quaint assemblage of European and American garb the two chiefs greatly enhanced their feeling of importance.[1]

[1] "Afternoon at Moroto," in *Atlantic Monthly*, January, 1960, pp. 37-38.

On occasion we see small boys stalking about impressively on stilts. They live in an adult world. Everywhere grown-ups tower over them. They yearn for the time when they too will be grown-ups. Hence, to get up on stilts and stand higher than the tallest man on the street yields a piquant satisfaction not unlike an ice-cream cone on a hot afternoon. In each case the sensation is fleeting but, for the moment, how delicious!

Consequently, it is no surprise to come upon evidence of it in the New Testament. On at least one occasion it came to the surface among the disciples and our Lord dealt with it. "Whoever would be great among you," he declared, "must be your servant." Do you want to be important? Then forget yourself in kindly concern for the well-being of others. Do you want to make "Who's Who" in the kingdom of God? Then lose yourself for the good of others.

Since this seems to be a revolutionary requirement, contrary to nature, our Lord has given us an example. The classic illustration, of course, is the memorable incident which occurred during the Last Supper.

When the twelve gathered with him in the upper room of the Jerusalem home where arrangments had been made for their supper, nothing had been going well. Rosy dreams of success were fast being swallowed up by humiliating and foreboding defeat. Their leader, once the idol of the crowds, now was denounced as subversive. Charges of blasphemy and treachery were leveled against him. Once they had felt proud and important when people pointed, saying, "He's a follower of the Galilean." Now, this made them squirm in embarrassment and fear. So they entered the room that night apprehensive, edgy, each wrapped in his own thoughts and fears, each wondering how he was going to save his own skin.

Of a consequence, common courtesies customarily practiced on such occasions were neglected. Usually there had been good-natured rivalry as to who would serve the others. But that night, not so.

On a stand nearby was the basin with water and towels. Since people of that time wore open sandals and traveled mostly on foot over hot and dusty roads, it was customary, immediately upon arrival, for a servant to remove a guest's sandals and bathe his feet and ankles in cool water. No doubt this was a kindness the disciples had happily done for one another, much as today we help a friend remove his overcoat or carry his bag to the guest room. But this evening the towel and basin stood untouched.

No one had volunteered. All sat stiff, silent, unyielding. Our Lord, as was his custom, broke the bread and blessed it. So the meal began in silence—a silence ugly with selfish thoughts, ambitions, and fears.

The Master knew what was in their hearts. Quietly slipping from his place, he laid aside his outer garments, and girded himself with a towel. Pouring water into the basin, he knelt beside the first man, silently bathed his feet and wiped them with the towel. Then he went to the next, and the next, and the next. The silence continued, broken only by the gentle sound of fresh water being poured into the basin.

They had stopped eating. Each was staring down into his plate, ashamed to look at the others. Finally our Lord came to Peter. Seeing the Master kneeling at his feet, the big fisherman could stand it no longer. Leaping up, he cried out, "You shall never wash my feet." But Jesus answered, "If I do not wash you, you have no part in me." Whereupon Peter, in shame and remorse, sobbed, "Lord, not my feet only but also my hands and my head!"

When he had finished with the last man, including Judas, Jesus stood and said to them as to us, "I have given you an example."

"Whoever would be great among you must be your servant . . . even as the Son of man came not to be served but to serve." It is a revolutionary requirement, but we have an Example who speaks for truth which cannot be denied.

This truth is supported not only in the example of him who through self-forgetting service became the greatest among men, but by personal experience.

Life, we discover, is a carbon copy of our Lord's parable about the grain of wheat. The grain of wheat which remains in the granary lives only unto itself. No demands are made of it. No sacrifice is required of it. It lives for itself, enjoys itself, serves itself. But as years pass, slowly it shrivels. The mysterious essence of life deeply hidden within dies. In the end it is worthless dust. How different the destiny of wheat seed that is taken from the granary and planted! It must abandon self-comfort and be subjected to the loneliness and darkness of earth, the cold and wet of rain. It must risk peril: birds may steal it, worms devour it, animals trample it, or wheels of machinery crush it. It must lose itself, die to itself, to be of service to others. But out of such self-surrender in service comes its beauty and its bounty.

Life is just like that, said Jesus. "Unless a grain of wheat falls into the earth and dies, it remains alone; but if it dies, it bears much fruit." "Whoever would save his life will lose it; and who ever loses his life for my sake and the gospel's will save it."

So long as we are wrapped up in self-concern, our best self is in chains. We are inhibited, frustrated, condemned to a life sentence behind prison walls of pettiness and mediocrity. We are like a plane lumbering awkwardly down the runway, wanting to fly yet unable to get off the ground. But once we lose ourselves in loving service of a noble ideal, a great cause, a worthy leader, especially that represented in Christ, suddenly we are free, airborne! We are bound yet gloriously free. "In his service is perfect freedom."

Rather than begrudge the summons to work, serve, and give through the church or complain against the duties of family and community, let us thank God and answer it with glad hearts. This is the key which unlocks the prison door and gives freedom to our best.

Come farther now to see that in the self-forgetting service of which our Lord has set the example we not only gain freedom but make for harmony and happiness.

Self-seeking creates conflict within and without. Every instance recorded in the Gospels of strife among the disciples grew out of contention about place and position. Excessive self-concern always engenders strife whether in home, church, industry, or among the nations. And it feeds the heart a witch's brew.

On the other hand, however, what does more to make for harmony and happiness than the bigness of kindly concern for others, concern expressed in self-forgetting service. What a spring of pure joy for heart and home, marriage and church! It is the sparkling sun and soaking rain of spring that makes the seeds of justice, mercy, hope, and peace grow among men and nations.

In reading the history of civilizations, again and again one comes upon descriptions of ancient conquests and mighty triumphs. Entire nations were reduced to servitude, hundreds of thousands among the vanquished sold into slavery, other hundreds of thousands worked under the lash to build enormous monuments in stone to their conquerors. Victory processions were lavish spectacles of greed and cruelty. Trumpeters usually led the march, after them followed floats representing captured cities. Then came wagons and carts loaded with loot—gold, silver, works of art, treasures of every kind—stripped from the vanquished. After them trudged the royalty and other leaders of the defeated who yet remained alive, especially the conquered king and his sons, his wife, and daughters—the latter already assigned to the conqueror's harem. Then last, in a gleaming chariot preceded by incense bearers and musicians, came the great man himself wearing the emblems of victory and followed by his troops.

It was a scene the ancient world knew all too well. Never were the victors long secure and never did the wine of success long remain sweet to their taste. Always their thirst remained unquenched and always the violence of their striving became a sword for their own death. That of which they dreamed and for which they suffered and tortured and killed long since has fallen into shabby ruins and become mounds for the grazing of goats.

But amidst the dark cruelty of those bitter years there

came forth One who spent himself in love, doing good; who took a towel with a basin and knelt to wash his followers' feet; who went to a cross for your sins and mine. He assembled no armies, smashed no cities, exacted no tribute. He came, he said, "not to be served, but to serve." So men have found him the way, the truth, and the life. To remember him is to love him; to love him is to worship him; to worship him is to serve him; to serve him is to serve one another in his spirit; and so to serve is to yield the fruits of peace and of joy!

Will Durant tells of Mycenae, which fourteen centuries before Christ was an awesome citadel, greatest capital of prehistoric Greece. Through the centuries it continued to flourish and wax mighty. During the sixth century, B.C., Homer could describe it as "a well-built city, broad avenued and abounding in gold."

But eventually, as do all works of man's pride and selfish striving, it fell. Its streets ran with blood and echoed to cries of grief and terror. Then, through a hundred generations, its ruins slept until uncovered by archaeologists. In a corner of its ancient wall has been found the famous Lion Gate. There, says Durant, "Carved upon a stone triangle over a massive lintel, two royal beasts, now worn and headless, dumbly stand guard over a grandeur that is gone." [2] But, he adds, "Standing on the ruins of Mycenae, one sees, in the little village below, a modest Christian church. Grandeur is gone; simplicity and consolation remain. Civiliza-

[2] *The Life of Greece* ("The Story of Civilization," Vol. II [New York: Simon and Schuster, 1939]), p. 28.

tions come and go; they conquer the earth and crumble into dust; but faith survives every desolation." [3]

The works of pride deceive and destroy us, but the works of love abide to heal and to bless.

We want to be important; this is as normal as breathing. Then let us remember him who girded himself with a towel and knelt to wash his followers' feet and then said, "I have given you an example."

[3] *Ibid.*, pp. 32, 33.

chapter seven

WHAT TO DO
WHEN DRAFTED

SOME TIME AGO, WHEN INVITED TO CONDUCT PREACHING
missions at air force bases in the Far East, I wrote a previous
missioner for advice. "Remember they are just typical boys,
very young," he counseled, "eight to ten thousand miles
from home; none wanting to be where he is; each yearning
to be in the corner drugstore back home."

Millions of youth feel themselves to be victims of titanic,
irrational, and evil forces; helpless pawns shoved where they
do not want to go, required to undergo loneliness, hardship,
and danger they did not elect, live under threat of disaster
they did not design.

But as we know this is more than a problem for youth
under compulsion of military service. It is a hard and stub-
born fact, a thorn in the flesh we all come to know. Soon
or late everyone is drafted for service not his choosing, conscripted by ugly and irrational circumstance.

Trouble comes like a thief in the night, worst of all is
trouble which is not our fault. Cherished hopes must be
scuttled, careful plans abandoned. Security is lost in chaos;
comfort in travail. Anguish is our wages; pain our reward.

In rain and gathering gloom a crowded train pulls out

from the Union Station in Los Angeles. It is bound for San Diego but its destination—tragedy. Scarcely beyond the city limits it becomes a shambles of tangled steel and tortured flesh.

An airliner, loaded to capacity with servicemen returning from Asia for Christmas at home, flounders after a takeoff at Seattle and falls to earth, a flaming grave.

A man tours the local bars until liquor has robbed him of restraint and decency, reduced him to a beast. Near midnight he returns home in a raging fury, beats his wife, pursues her about the house as she flees desperately for her life, and finally kills her on their front lawn. Their terrified children watch in frozen horror. That night of terror and its immeasurable, crippling consequences will be with them all their days.

Children are robbed of their parents; a lovely young woman is mutilated for life by a maniac; a father's capacity to support his family is destroyed by a drinking driver— some "man of distinction." Such things happen every day. We read about them occurring in distant places, involving people we do not know, and they bounce from our armor. We shrug off a momentary feeling of regret and pity and go on our way. But when calamity strikes close to home, then a jagged question is driven into the heart. "Why?" we ask, "Why should that be allowed to happen? Why should the innocent be made to suffer?"

This is a world in which a Socrates may be required to drink hemlock, a Stephen is stoned, a Paul beheaded, a Lincoln shot, and Jesus Christ sent to a cross. This is a world in which innocent and helpless people may be driven from their homes into squalor, starvation, and terror by war. This is a world in which the helpless and innocent may be conscripted by dark and crippling circumstance.

In this world there is injustice. The innocent suffer. Love is betrayed. Righteousness goes unrewarded. Truth is persecuted. Prophets are stoned. Saints are slain. That is hard, jagged truth; a thorn which pierces the flesh and spirit of us all, sooner or later.

How do we react to it, think about it, live with it? When fell circumstance suddenly conscripts us for unwilling service, what should we do about it? That is the question.

The classic treatment of this problem is the Old Testament poem known as the Book of Job. A literary masterpiece ranking with Dante's *Divine Comedy* and Milton's *Paradise Lost*, Job is perhaps the most original work in all literature.

The prologue states the problem: "There was a man in the land of Uz, whose name was Job;" it begins, "and that man was blameless and upright, one who feared God, and turned away from evil."

He was "blameless." According to the Hebrew source, it means he was a man of mental and physical health; a sound, well-rounded, self-possessed, competent person. He was "upright," a man straightforward and just in all his dealings. Even his wife bore testimony of his integrity. He was a man of sincere piety and high morality.

He was blessed, we are told, with a large and happy family. In those unenlightened days, a man's good fortune was measured by sons, not daughters. Job had seven sons, three daughters. It was a harmonious household. Parents and children enjoyed each other's company. What is more, it was a deeply religious household. Job had concern not only for his children's outward performance of religious disciplines but for what they thought of God in their hearts.

In addition, Job had prospered. He was a man of great enterprises and vast wealth.

To round out perfection, Job enjoyed not only health, a large and happy family, and great wealth, but also the satisfactions of social esteem. He was accorded great honor and deeply beloved by all, lowly and mighty alike.

Then the writer shifts the scene to heaven. The sons of God, together with Satan, presented themselves before the Lord.

The Lord said to Satan, "Whence have you come?" Satan answered the Lord, "From going to and fro on the earth, and from walking up and down on it." And the Lord said to Satan, "Have you considered my servant Job, that there is none like him on the earth, a blameless and upright man, who fears God and turns away from evil?" Then Satan answered the Lord, "Does Job fear God for nought? Hast thou not put a hedge about him and his house and all that he has, on every side? Thou hast blessed the work of his hands, and his possessions have increased in the land. But put forth thy hand now, and touch all that he has, and he will curse thee to thy face." And the Lord said to Satan, "Behold, all that he has is in your power."

The Lord posted one reservation; do not hurt his person.

So Satan returned to the earth. On a day of feasting word came to Job that all his possessions had been destroyed, then that his sons and daughters had been killed.

Job was stripped of all he had, reduced to penury, and left childless. But Job said, "Naked I came from my mother's womb, and naked shall I return; the Lord gave, and the Lord has taken away; blessed be the name of the Lord."

Came the day when Satan and the Lord had another meeting in heaven.

The Lord said to Satan, "Have you considered my servant Job, that there is none like him on the earth. . . . He still holds fast his integrity, although you moved me against him, to destroy him without cause." Then Satan answered the Lord, "Skin for skin! All that a man has he will give for his life. But put forth thy hand now, and touch his bone and his flesh, and he will curse thee to thy face." And the Lord said to Satan, "Behold, he is in your power; only spare his life."

Satan again visited the earth. Soon Job was afflicted by disease worse than death. He was exiled to the village garbage dump, there to sit amid rotting refuse, rats, and homeless dogs and await death. His wife, who alone of his household had survived, urged him to curse God and take his life.

Here at last three old and wise friends found him. And here they grappled with the age-old question: Why should a man like Job come to such an end? "My God, why?"

Consider now the answer they gave, that which Job at last accepted, and finally that which is found in Christianity.

The writer uses each of Job's friends to voice the orthodox answer given by the ancient world to the problem of suffering. That answer was: all suffering is the consequence of sin, just punishment for sin; righteousness is rewarded by exemption from trouble and pain. Therefore, should an apparently righteous man be overtaken by calamity, this is merely evidence that he either is not or has not been so righteous as he appears. He is in truth a sinner receiving just punishment.

Hence, Job's friends said, "Though embarrassing to admit, Job, the plain truth is, you are getting what you deserve. Either consciously or unconsciously, you have sinned. Therefore, the omnipotent and inescapable justice of God has overtaken you. Accept your punishment in good grace and commit your way unto God."

"You are dead wrong," answered Job. "Granted that I, being a mortal man, am not sinless; still in the name of justice and reason, I have done nothing to deserve such punishment."

"Your theory does not meet the test of facts," Job insisted. "It is plain as day that the righteous as well as the wicked often suffer, indeed sometimes the wicked prosper and enjoy life while the righteous are crushed under adversity. To be a just and upright man does not bring immunity from trouble in this world."

Still there are those who cling to the opinion that only the sinful suffer, that to be righteous buys immunity from trouble and suffering. Still it is theory denied by facts. Now as then, to assume that a good man overtaken by calamity is being punished for reason of secret and heinous sins not only violates truth but cruelly multiplies his anguish.

Job at last arrived at another answer. The problem created by the fact of suffering by the righteous, he affirmed, is beyond the reach of man's mind. Man is incapable of arriving at a rational solution. Nevertheless, no matter what, Job said, I will trust in God. "Though he slay me," as the King James Version magnificently puts it, "yet will I trust in him."

> I know that my Redeemer lives,
>   and at last he will stand upon the earth; . . .
> whom I shall see on my side.

So Job at last came to peace in his controversy with his friends, with God, and with his troubles. The ancient writer attached an epilogue which gives a happy ending. God rebuked Job's misguided friends and blessed Job anew. Indeed, God gave him once again seven sons and three daughters, doubled the wealth he once enjoyed, and restored him to a place of honor. But all of that, while pleasant to contemplate, is quite beside the point. Job's supreme achievement was his arrival at the place where he could accept his afflictions without rebellion and self-pity. Though still unable, in justice, to find a reason for them, he trusted utterly in God, confident that in the end he would see that God was on his side, serving his good.

This is an honest answer to the problem of suffering that does justice to facts. In it a person overtaken by the slings and arrows of misfortune can find comfort and take courage.

A small girl riding her bicycle pell-mell down a gravel road takes a header over the handlebars. Hands, arms, face, and knees are lacerated. The wounds are filled with dirt and gravel. At first she is stunned and feels little pain. By the time she reaches home she is miserable. Her injuries will not prove fatal. She will live to ride again. But when her father begins to wash away the dirt and apply an antiseptic, the torment truly begins. She screams and tries to pull away. She knows nothing of the danger of infection. If she does she has forgotten it. Gradually through the turbulence of her pain, she sees her father's face and is reassured. She realizes her father is on her side, that in the end she will have reason to know it. She cannot understand why she must suffer the added torment of cleansing and disinfecting her wounds, but she trusts her father. In this trust she finds inner steadiness and courage. Sobs may yet rack her body, but she stands up and takes it!

Such is the answer Job gave to suffering. There is value in it.

But there is a nobler and wiser answer to the problem of suffering. It is that which is represented by the Cross. When overtaken by adversity you do not deserve, do more than accept it without self-pity and rebellion. Believe that God in mercy is with you and will help you use it for good.

No greater injustice was ever inflicted than that which nailed Jesus Christ upon a cross and left him to die as a common criminal. Then truly did the innocent suffer. But how he used that cross for good! Hence we place it on altars and on steeples and find it a window open wide toward the best we can know of God and the best we can hope for ourselves.

Paul translated this insight represented by the Cross into workable terms for application to our daily lives when he wrote: "We rejoice in our sufferings, knowing that suffering produces endurance, and endurance produces character, and character produces hope, and hope does not disappoint us, because God's love has been poured into our hearts."

A world which makes possible the growth of human beings requires freedom. A world which permits freedom makes suffering, even that of the innocent, inevitable. There is no way to have a safe, snug, comfortable world which shuts out all possibility of trouble and pain and at the same time have a world which provides human beings with opportunity for growth toward maturity and fulfillment, all that is meant by life as exemplified supremely by Jesus Christ.

But as the Cross reminds us, suffering need not have the last word. It can be made a servant for good, even greatest good. For example, says Paul, God is present with us in our suffering and will help us use it for creating a noble life.

A stranger driving past a church building site may look up and see only a forest of raw lumber rising. It is awkward, ungainly, and ugly to look upon. It has been erected at some expense. But those who share the enterprise know it is merely a temporary necessity. Once the great columns are erected, the roof sections hoisted into position, and the concrete poured and stressed, then the scaffolding will come down and all will see taking form a magnificent temple that for generations will serve men for God and invite men to God.

Thus trouble and suffering, even for the innocent, may in God's grace be scaffolding by which the immortal temple of the soul is reared.

We may not like the scaffolding, but the fact remains that it is a necessity for the building. We do not begin life with personality and character complete. We are provided with land, material, and a proved set of plans. The work of building is our assignment. Such building requires the scaffolding of trouble, even suffering of the innocent. There is no other way for the building to rise.

A teacher of mine once said, "While perfected souls may some day live in a perfected world called heaven, there is no way to make them except in an imperfect world like this. Character cannot be created by command nor saints by fiat. Heaven is gained at the end of the journey, not at the beginning, and the way between is hard and grievous."

That is the way things are and must be. The immortal Homer bears witness. Remember the incident? The Greeks, coming home from their long and victorious Trojan wars, grew weary of the hard-handled oars, the ceaseless pounding of the sea, and relentless sun, the stern struggle against storms. So they rested themselves on the island of the Lotus Eaters. There they found what they assumed was Paradise, a shortcut to heaven.

But without struggle their paradise became a pigsty and they its swine. Without the buffeting and pain of trouble there can only be swine, not saints; cabbages, not character. We enter the kingdom of God, says Jesus, by way of tribulation. There is no other way.

Supremely the Cross assures us that we do not suffer alone—never! It declares that God is not a spectator, viewing our travail from a safe and comfortable seat on the rim of the cosmos. Rather, it says God is here with us, sharing our lot; that whatever life requires of us, he pays with us; that whatever cup of suffering is given us, he drinks with us to the last bitter dregs. This makes a difference, a redeeming difference.

Once a little boy was badly injured. Those who cared for him had to hurt him even more. He was in a strange and frightening place surrounded by strange and frightening people. His pain was terrible, and he was terrified. All he could do was call for his mother. "Mother! Mother! Oh, Mother, Mother!" he wailed. His cries echoed through the building and down the street. It was enough to tear one's heart in two.

Then at last his mother was found and brought to his cot. She sat there beside him and let him grip her hand. She placed another hand upon his forehead and spoke quietly to him. Gradually terror left his eyes and he lay quiet, bearing his pain like a man. Knowing he did not suffer alone, that someone who loved him was with him, brought comfort and courage.

Even so, when suffering is our lot, when pain is a demon, and terror lurks around a corner, the Cross has something to say to us. We are reminded that we are not alone. We know Someone who understands and loves us is by our side, taking us by the hand, sharing our plight. So we can bear our pain like men.

Surely the prize news story recently was that of the man who came to life in a hearse. His wife thought he was dead, the ambulance crew thought he was dead, the doctor thought he was dead, the men sent by the mortuary thought he was dead. Everybody thought he was dead—maybe he did, too. But halfway to the mortuary the driver of the hearse and his assistant thought they heard a strange noise. Was it the traffic? Somebody passing by? Or just their imagination? It couldn't be the corpse, they thought.

75

At last they stopped the hearse and one of them said, "Let's see what's what here!"

At last report the man is now up and walking about and says he wants to go to work again.

The problem of suffering, especially when involving the innocent, is a thorny question. For this there are no smooth and easy answers. We can be sure, however, even when we fail to find the reason in justice, that we are not being punished by a wrathful God. Though we may not be able to understand why we should be conscripted for service of fell circumstance, at least like Job we can believe that God is alive, that we have a Redeemer, and that in the end we will know he has been serving our good.

Better still, we can learn from the Cross there is with us a God of love, sharing our plight, and enabling us to make even the worst a servant of the best.

Then truly we can be like the man thought dead who comes to life!

chapter eight

A SON GONE WRONG

THEY STOOD IN THE COURTROOM TOGETHER, FATHER AND
son. The father, distinguished of bearing and prominent in
his profession, was crushed under remorse and shame. His
heart cried out in pity and penitence for the lad, a son
gone wrong. For him death would have worn a welcome
face. The lad, half boy and half man, richly endowed of
mind and body, showed no sign of regret or desire for
pardon. Hostile, arrogant, and defiant, he was at war against
all, even his father.

To see them was to remember the grief of David over
Absalom—"And the king was deeply moved, and went up
to the chamber over the gate, and wept; and as he went, he
said, 'O my son Absalom, my son, my son Absalom! Would
I had died instead of you, O Absalom, my son, my son!' "

So David, king of Israel, lamented the death of a son.
But death was the least of it. Absalom had been the apple
of his eye, a lad of great promise. Handsome, virile, dash-
ing, winsome; as the Bible tells it. "In all Israel there was
no one so much to be praised for his beauty as Absalom;
from the sole of his foot to the crown of his head there
was no blemish in him."

David had seen in Absalom the promise of greatness, potential which would make him worthy the throne of Israel, a king who would lead the young nation's continuing march to power and prosperity when he had been gathered to his fathers. David had looked upon him with a proud and loving heart. All his achievements of the past and hopes for the future would be safe, he had believed, in the keeping of Absalom.

But Absalom turned sullen and resentful. He had rebellion in his heart. He used his position of trust and prestige to conspire against his father, exploiting discontent among the people. He posed as the friend and champion of all who felt themselves wronged, hinting that the king was indifferent to their plight. He would say to those aggrieved, "Of course your claims are good and right, but the king has no deputy to hear you. O that I were a judge in the land! Then you would have justice." Absalom went about with cunning, stealing the hearts of the people away from his father. The conspiracy grew. Finally Absalom, under pretense of going to Hebron on a religious pilgrimage, dared have himself there annointed king of Israel. Then with an army he marched on Jerusalem to take the throne.

David was caught completely by surprise. No doubt he had heard rumors of Absalom's misbehavior, but had not been able to believe them, at least not to take them seriously. David with his bodyguard fled for his life. Absalom entered Jerusalem in triumph. With his followers he pursued David into the wilderness beyond Jordan. David quickly gained supporters and a fighting force. As the hosts of Absalom drew near and battle was imminent, David, still the compassionate father, summoned his officers and said, "Deal gently for my sake with the young man Absalom."

The battle was fought in the forest of Ephraim. The army of Absalom was routed and scattered, crushed with a slaughter of more than twenty thousand men. In the confusion Absalom, riding furiously, passed under a great oak tree. There was clearance for the mule, but not for Absalom. Absalom's head was caught within the boughs. The mule went racing on. Absalom remained with the tree, dangling helpless between heaven and earth. There David's men found him, and, despite the king's plea, there Absalom was killed.

But some things are worse than death, worse than loss of every treasure earth can give. David had won his way from a shepherd's tent to a palace. He had delivered a young, weak nation from disunity and defeat. He had won victories in war and by diplomacy unrivaled in the history of his people. He had led Israel into strength and wealth never known before, gaining personal glory, honor, and riches. Now word had come of victory that had ended a rebellion and restored unity in the realm. For David, however, that was ashes. All was destroyed by knowledge of Absalom's sin and disgrace now made final by death, scourging evidence of his failure as a father.

He would rather have died than see such a day. Death would have been sweet. Bent under shame and remorse, great King David turned from his men and climbed the stairs to a lonely chamber above the city's gates, sobbing as he went: "O my son Absalom, my son, my son Absalom! Would I had died instead of you, O Absalom, my son, my son!"

How oft repeated that tragedy! In our greatest city a grand jury recently recommended that an armed policeman be stationed in every school. Juvenile violence and crime across the nation has climbed to frightening new records year after year. According to federal statistics, for instance, 34,599 "children under 18" were arrested by police in 1950; whereas in 1958 the number of "children under 18" arrested by police was 284,215—an increase of nearly eight times over a period of eight years! [1]

Every such youth is to some degree an Absalom. And all who bear adult responsibility for them—parents, school, church, society as a whole—share in some degree the failure and shame of David.

What makes an Absalom? Why do youth go wrong? What can be done? There are no stock answers, no easy solutions. But we are required to try. What matters our high standard of living, our material progress, even the launching of man-made satellites, if decay among our youth continues to increase! What matter the triumphs of David and the prosperity of Israel, if there be the tragic waste of an Absalom!

What makes an Absalom? Several causes stand out in the ancient story and are no less present today.

Consider one of the more prominent; that is, an environment which hinders growth into maturity. That was the plight of Absalom. It is the plight of most American youth today.

Review what is involved in the business of growing up,

[1] *Statistical Abstract of the United States,* 1960 (U. S. Department of Commerce, Bureau of the Census), p. 143.

achieving maturity. H. A. Overstreet, in a splendid book dealing with this matter, describes our starting point and our goals.[2]

An infant, he says, with the strength and authority of a man, would be a monster. He has no knowledge; therefore, his acts of power would be acts of ignorance. He is completely ego-centered; therefore, his acts of power would be aimed solely at self-gratification. He has no awareness of the needs, rights, and feelings of others; therefore, his acts of power would be often acts of cruelty. He has no sense of responsibility; therefore, his acts of power would be acts of whim. He has no appreciation of the toil, skill, concern, and sacrifice by which others have provided for him; therefore his acts of power would often be destructive.[3]

There we all begin. There we start together in the business of growing up, gaining or developing the qualities which constitute "maturity."

What are the marks of a mature person? What are the goals toward which we should grow? Overstreet lists a number. They long have been universally known and esteemed. What is a mature human being?

1. He is a person whose understanding keeps pace with his increasing powers; who grows in his ability to discern the excellent and relate the particular to the whole; whose knowledge of the past serves the present and improves the future. He is a person of purpose, perspective, poise, and competence.

2. He is a person who has developed his capacity for

[2] *The Mature Mind* (New York: W. W. Norton & Company, 1949); see especially chapters 2, 3, and 10.
[3] *Ibid.*, pp. 43, 44.

empathy, what Dr. Overstreet calls "social imagination." He has learned to think and to act in awareness of the needs, rights, and feelings of others. He puts himself in the other fellow's shoes, looks out at life through his eyes.

3. He is a person who accepts responsibility commensurate with his powers. He accepts the fact that he is a part of the human family and acts accordingly. He respects and obeys laws necessary for the common good. He willingly bears burdens, serves duty, and denies self in the interest of the common good.

4. He has inner control. He keeps the bridle on his "animal drives" and directs them toward worthy goals. He is a person who has acquired resources for, and develops self-discipline in, the practice of inner control.

These, we would agree with Dr. Overstreet, are among the chief qualities of maturity. Others, could be mentioned. They are all put together incomparably in the person of Jesus Christ. He was the most mature person who ever lived on the earth. In him we see most clearly and completely the dimensions of maturity, the goals which tell the reason for our being alive.

Obviously, the environment of Absalom as a prince in the house of Israel handicapped his growth into maturity. David, of course, failed to know this—at least not in time. No doubt often he looked upon Absalom and thought: "How much better is his lot than was mine as a lad. For him there are no lonely shepherd's vigils through dark and stormy nights; no terrifying encounters with wild beasts; no long, exhausting treks through the wilderness in search of lost sheep. For him there is no menial labor, no grinding monotony of daily chores, no poverty, no lowly state.

He's a prince in the house of Israel, an heir to the throne. He has everything." Little did David realize then that as a shepherd lad he had a far better climate for becoming a man; that Absalom's celebrated privileges were in reality handicaps. That was the predicament of Absalom, 1000 B.C.

It is no less the predicament of most American youth, late twentieth century. One hundred years ago most of America lived on farms or in small towns. Beginning at the age of five or six most boys and girls began to share some responsibility for the well-being of their home. They had chores to perform, errands to run, work to do. As they grew older their responsibilities increased. Should they neglect them, they and all their household in some degree suffered. They were given a wholesome outlet for their energies; and in the case of boys, a healthful chance to play the man. They had space: room for yelling and running wild, room for privacy and quiet, too. They lived in the company of their father as well as of their mother. They watched him at work, helped him in his work, and felt as if they were on the team. Thus children and youth of the agrarian America of one hundred years ago were surrounded by constant incentive to grow in knowledge of what life is about, in sensitivity to and concern for the welfare of others, in capacity for an acceptance of responsibility, and in practice of inner control. They were reared in a climate conducive to growth and maturity.

Today most of America has moved from the country and small towns into cities and plush suburban communities. Children rarely see their father at work, to say nothing of helping him in his work. Many see little of their father at any time except on weekends. They have little or no knowledge of how the family is supported. They have little or nothing of any significance to do for the family.

We live in a gadget culture, a push-button age. We delight in comforts and luxuries beyond the dreams of kings and potentates one hundred years ago. This is pleasant for adults—and no doubt heaven for housewives—but for teen-agers, especially teen-age boys, in many respects it is hell—a nice, chrome-plated, neon-lighted, vitamin-stocked, electronic, push-button, air-conditioned hell! Like Absalom, they are all princes in the house of Israel. They have everything, everything but what they most need for the business of growing up.

Let me speak of boys and teen-age young men in particular; for they, I do believe, are most handicapped by modern culture. They want to become manly. Though they are often confused as to what this means, it represents their chief ambition. For this they need to learn what life is about and what real manhood is from a day-by-day, man-to-man relationship with their father, working at his side if possible, sharing some of his burden. They need responsibilities which waken them to concern for the welfare of others, which make them know they are important and trusted, an asset to the family and community. They need hard tasks which demand skill and pluck, self-reliance and persistence. They need obligations which school them in respect for authority and the practice of self-control. In short, they need a chance to play the man. Today that chance is sharply curtailed for the average youth in America.

Add to this other negative factors characteristic of our times: the increasingly large number of mothers employed away from home, the high divorce rate, the neurotic obsession with sex, the inevitable moral deterioration caused by war, and a decade of nationwide hysteria coincident with the cold war! Little wonder that increasing numbers of youth go wrong. What could we expect!

What can we do?

We have responsibility as members of the community. We can understand the problem and co-operate with agencies which seek to provide in our contemporary culture adequate substitutes for the maturity incentives so characteristic of an agrarian culture, institutions such as Boy Scouts and the Y.M.C.A.

Also, as members of the community we can repent of the sins which create the moral climate that now blights our youth; not just the corporate sins of our times, but our own sins, our personal sins. And when some youth is in bad trouble, before calling for the judge to "throw the book" at him, let us first search our own hearts and then remember the woman flung at the Master's feet and hear him say, "He that is without sin among you, let him first cast a stone at her." (K.J.V.) There is need for punishment, yes. That too is a requirement for growing up. But let there be no self-righteous condemnation, no "holier-than-thou" strutting. Let there be the humility of shared guilt and of penitence.

We have responsibility as parents. David succeeded as a king and failed as a parent. He built a kingdom, but lost a son. Worse still, his own moral failures rose up to defeat him as a father. It was remorse for his failure as a father that made David wish for death. This was the failure which reduced all this triumphs to ashes.

No parent has more important business than, God helping, being the best kind of a parent he can become. Nothing can compensate for failure as a parent. To be faced
with evidence of such failure is anguish worse than death.
On the other hand, nothing can equal the rewards which
come to a successful parent and the lasting good achieved
for society.

Supremely, we have responsibility as youth. We are not
cabbages, helpless creatures of circumstance. We have the
final vote. We can decide for the right or the wrong. Everyone can choose which way his soul shall go.

Given the best of environment and the finest of parents
we still fight the battle with temptation, we still can surrender to evil. Even God himself cannot keep us from
taking the low road if that is what we decide to do. Despite
all, we can choose the way of evil, bringing disgrace and
injury to self and others.

Or, given the worst of environment and the poorest of
parents, we can grow, God helping, toward the likeness of
Jesus Christ. Many have! Many do!

Let no youth pass off the blame for his wrongdoing to
the inadequacy of his environment or to the failures of his
parents. The unlimited redemptive resources of Almighty
God are open to him. He can choose to grow like Jesus
Christ if he will. The last and deciding vote is his own.

What makes an Absalom? Why do youth go wrong?
There are no doctrinaire answers, no easy solutions. But
each of us in his own area of responsibility must try. And
for him who tries, God stands at his shoulder.

chapter nine

IS PURITY PASSÉ?

Is purity passé? outmoded? gauche?

We read in the Ten Commandments: "You shall not commit adultery." Jesus Christ lifted that moral standard even higher. In the Sermon on the Mount we read: "You have heard that it was said, 'You shall not commit adultery.' But I say to you that every one who looks at a woman lustfully has already committed adultery with her in his heart."

There shall be purity in relationships between men and women, both in thought and deed. This is basic in Judaeo-Christian morality; fundamental to Western culture, especially to the institutions of marriage, home, and family; and long regarded a distinction between civilized living and primitivism.

"Is this a mistake?" asked a college-age discussion group. Is the moral standard of sexual purity unrealistic, repressive, or as some would say, much ado about trivia? Does it place an unnecessary and crippling burden upon mankind? Is it a gloomy relic of the past, an ethical requirement no longer relevant? Is purity passé?

It is apparent many are of that opinion. Witness, for example, titles and pictures which adorn paperback books on display at newspaper stands in any airport, railway station, or bus depot. Read best-selling novels. Note movie advertisements, especially the torrid scenes in vivid color posted at the entrance of motion-picture theaters. Give thought to the fervid pleas and promises of many popular songs. Who are the most highly publicized Hollywood female stars? Are they actresses or bodies? It would seem that adultery in one form or another is our chief interest and occupation.

For anyone who would imagine this is but a bad dream, that sexual morality in our times has not been on the toboggan, there are the Kinsey reports. Granting that they may be based upon an inadequate sampling, cut their findings by 50 per cent. Still there would be reason for grave concern.

How did we arrive at this present contradiction? this disparity between long-hallowed moral law and present-day conduct?

Part of the blame, of course, must be placed upon wars, both hot and cold, of the past fifty years. Morality is the first casualty of war and the last to recover. The separations and loneliness; the alternation between worst monotony and wildest excitement; the philosophy of "Live it up today for tomorrow you may die"—all such physical and psychological abnormalities of wartime living tend to loosen the grip of morality. The surrender of moral standards which war requires weakens the overall authority of moral law. The denial of human worth required in mass killing of the enemy destroys the sense of chivalry, respect for womanhood, and reverence for the sanctity of marriage in the homeland as well as elsewhere. One cannot teach men to lie, steal, and kill under the requirements of war and not have many decide they may as well break the rest of the Ten Commandments; that to seduce a girl or another man's wife is of small consequence, something to be done "just for kicks."

Hence on the heels of World War I came the moral debacle of the 1920's, the jazz and flapper era; and following World War II with its ensuing cold war, our present obeisance at the shrine of Brigitte Bardot and Elvis Presley, et al.

No less responsibility for this assault upon morality must be laid at the door of modern urban living. The rural society once characteristic of America provided powerful incentives and controls for chastity in relationships between men and women.

There was permanence, stability. Once a family settled in a countryside or small town, it took root. People stayed put. Everyone knew everyone else. A good name in the community was a family's most prized possession. To maintain it was an urgent responsibility felt by every member of the family. That is motive for morality.

Urban life of today, however, is characterized by impermanence and the impersonal. We flit from place to place like the man on the flying trapeze. Thirty-five million Americans move to a new address each year, one fifth our total population. We live in an ocean of strange faces. The old monitor for righteousness, "What will the neighbors say?" has waned. Most of the exterior incentives and controls which helped our grandparents behave themselves are gone.

In horse-and-buggy days a young couple, as we have been

reminded, could never get so far away from home that someone would not recognize them, or at least the horse and buggy. By eight o'clock the next morning everyone in the neighborhood knew where Susie went, with whom she went, and when she got home. Today in fifteen minutes youth can be swallowed up in anonymity, among people who do not know them and do not care what they do so long as they do not make themselves obnoxious.

Urban living has taken down fences and weakened incentives which in other days made for purity in relationships between men and women.

Present-day life also has weakened the strength and influence of home and family life. The deep undergirding for good living once provided by old-fashioned homes is lacking in present-day society.

In addition are the frustrations, insecurities, tensions, and fears typical of modern urban life, conditions which invite the momentary escape, the narcotic afforded by sexual immorality.

The bitter fruits of war and those of drastic cultural change have brought upon us the moral decay reflected in the Kinsey reports. They have created a society quite as alien to the morality of purity taught by Jesus Christ in the Sermon on the Mount as was the pagan society of ancient Rome.

But no matter the trend of our times, reasons for purity are not passé. They are just as valid today as fifty years ago, as two thousand years ago.

We have to live with ourselves. The Christian moral code is not extraneous to us, an artificial requirement forced upon us. It is part of the warp and woof of our being, written in our flesh and spirit, in our nervous system and in every cell of our body, in our awareness of self and in our yearning for fellowship, both human and divine. It is the way we are meant to live. Violation of that code brings us into trouble, even as driving a car without oil burns out its bearings.

Hence, "You shall not commit adultery" is not an unnatural requirement for human beings. It would be if we were but animals, of course. But we are more than dogs and cats. Sex for human beings is more than a biological function; it is of the spirit, too. It involves our entire being. The Christian standard of chastity fulfills the need of our whole being. Anything less leaves us shoddy, soiled, cheated, and ashamed.

At first we may laugh off a violation of that code. But remembrance of that violation remains within us, deeply buried and festering. It will sicken and cripple us until repentance and divine forgiveness bring cleansing and release.

One universal reason for chastity is our need for self-respect, inner cleanness, and integrity. Each of us has to live with himself.

Also, sex is not a private affair. It involves others. The marriage ceremony is a symbol of that fact. It represents a contract we make in holy vows, not only with one another, but with society and with God.

Among pictures I once brought home from Asia was that of a lovely little girl, six years old, of wistful face and long, dark curls. Her mother is a young Japanese woman, the daughter of a Christian home, graduate of a Christian

college. On the back of the picture is the name of her father
and his last known address. He was an American officer of
high rank stationed in Tokyo.

It is the old story. The father and son of this Japanese
family were killed during the war. The mother and two
beautiful, gifted daughters were destitute, homeless, and
starving. The girls found employment in office work for
the American military forces. The younger daughter was
flattered by the attention of a handsome American officer.
He did not tell her he had a wife and family in San Fran-
cisco. She trusted him; fell in love with him; believed he
loved her and would marry her. Her family pleaded, but in
vain. Finally, to the shame of all, she lived with him. A
year passed. She became pregnant. He was rotated back
to the states and returned to civilian life. The old grand-
mother and young mother with the little child of the
American officer lived in a tiny, flimsy shelter near Tokyo,
desperately poor, of course. But that was nothing to them
compared with the deeper injury they suffered, the sense of
isolation and rejection, the shame and humiliation they will
bear until death. Sex is not a private affair. It deeply involves others.

Some years ago a man violated another man's home and
seduced his wife. Perhaps for him it was a casual matter,
just one more conquest to feed his ego, one more gay adventure. But the woman suffered deep emotional shock and
has required psychiatric treatment. She still is not well. For
fifteen years every member of her family has suffered in
consequence: her children, her husband, her parents. Sex
is not a private affair. It deeply involves others, many
others. Violation of the moral code inflicts upon them

injury no human being has the right to bring upon another.

Still another reason for purity is found in our expectations and obligations in marriage.

Violation of the moral code prior to marriage blights and cheapens the marriage relationship. The bride walks up an aisle to meet her betrothed at an altar. She is clothed in white, symbol of purity. This is not a casual tradition. A bride who comes to her wedding without the inner radiance, self-respect, and integrity symbolized by her dress has cheated herself of treasure beyond price. She has cheated her husband, too. What man worthy of the name wants to know that the bride moving up the aisle to stand with him is shoddy goods, a hand-me-down? And what he expects of his bride he should be honorable enough to offer in himself.

Violation of the moral code after marriage likewise blights and impoverishes the relationship; furthermore, it places the home itself in jeopardy.

Anthropologists agree that fidelity in marriage is one of the chief bulwarks of any social structure. Without it the rich fulfillment of marriage is denied and children are deprived emotional security to which they are entitled. Infidelity is legal ground for divorce in every state of the union.

Let no one imagine fidelity applies only to his deeds. A man who is mentally unfaithful to his wife, who permits himself to indulge in day dreams of promiscuity, who toys with the thought of seducing every woman attractive to him, is as destructive of his marriage as the man who is physically unfaithful. He is unable to give himself fully and sincerely to his wife. And his wife, though not consciously aware of his thoughts, feels insecure in the marriage. Unknowingly, she draws back, fearful of giving herself without reserve. Without doubt, mental unfaithfulness, though hidden, is a major cause of marital disappointment and discord.

Whatever may be the trend of our times, reasons for purity are not passé!

Now we come to the crux of our need. How do we strengthen commitment to purity?

First, we must guard our minds. Our minds quickly develop perverted appetites for filth. The story is told of a test pilot who dove a jet thirty thousand feet. When he pulled out, all his sins flashed before his eyes. Whereupon, he went back for six more dives.

Evil enters by way of the mind. First the evil thought, then the sinful deed. "For as he [a man] thinketh in his heart, so is he." (K.J.V.) If we have respect for our stomach and concern for our health we do not drink the contents of cesspools and eat garbage. Some books and pictures, stage shows and stories, are garbage, sewage. Feeding them to our mind makes us sick. We develop an appetite for filth and the sickness worsens.

Purity of life must begin in purity of mind. "Whatsoever things are true, . . . honest, . . . just, . . . pure, . . .; think on these things." (K.J.V.)

Second, we must guard our action. We should be alert to avoid conduct and situations that trigger the avalanche of passion.

Human emotion is a wondrous gift. But once out of

control, it is a savage power, heedless of morals or mercy, devastating as an avalanche.

Purity of life begins in the mind, but it is safeguarded by wise action. Refrain from conduct and avoid situations which trigger the fury of passion.

Third, remember you are trusted. There is an old hymn we would do well to recall every day:

> I would be true, for there are those who trust me;
> I would be pure, for there are those who care.

When tempted, think of all who trust you. Purity of life begins in the mind; it is safeguarded by wise action, and it is supported by remembering, "There are those who trust me."

Fourth, pray. Prayer is the shining armor, the weapon invincible. We are never tempted beyond our strength, if—we pray. Prayer purifies the mind and reinforces the will for righteousness. Prayer recovers ideals and develops strength for their service. Prayer delivers us from the blindness and folly of self and links us with the wisdom and power of God. The hosts of evil meet their match in a man on his knees.

> Lord, what a change within us one short hour
> Spent in Thy presence will prevail to make!
> .   .   .   .
> We kneel, how weak! We rise, how full of power!
> Why, therefore, should we do ourselves this wrong,
> Or others, that we are not always strong,

. . . .

When with us is prayer,
And joy and strength and courage are with Thee!
—RICHARD CHENEVIX TRENCH

Is purity passé?

Without it life becomes drab as a dusty road, disappointing as an empty well, messy as a barnyard. With it there is joy and strength, release and fulfillment.

chapter ten

CAN YOU LIVE WITH
ARITHMETIC?

WITH THE COMING OF AUTUMN, MOST SMALL BOYS DEVELOP
strong opinions about arithmetic. All summer they have
been dreading the worst. Now they know their fears were
not in vain. With shoulders tender under the hard scho-
lastic collar, they squirm, chafe, and fervently wish, "Oh,
if only I could get out of arithmetic."

But they know it is like wishing for Christmas twice a
year or for candy bars to pop up like dandelions. With
dragging feet they resign themselves to knowing that
arithmetic, like scrubbed ears, collars, and neckties, is their
inevitable plight.

By the time most small boys become grown men, however, they have so thoroughly capitulated to arithmetic, they
need to be delivered from it. They require such a deliverance lest they destroy their humanity and make the earth
a shabby, sterile, and shameful place.

Who in his better moments has not held suspect claims
made in behalf of "Now, be practical"? Who has not
questioned its assumptions of omniscience and yearned
for deliverance from its tyranny?

This was the rescue attempted in what happened long

ago at Bethany. Jesus was much beloved in that village close by Jerusalem and often visited friends there. On an evening just before his arrest, he was entertained at a dinner in his honor at the home of Simon. Everything went forward sedately according to plan until unexpectedly a woman burst into the room. To everyone's surprise she went directly to the guest of honor, broke open an alabaster jar of most expensive perfume, and poured it out upon his head, as was the custom for annointing a king. The perfume was worth the equivalent of a year's wages. It represented, no doubt, the most precious possession she would ever have. And she did not sprinkle just a few drops upon him; in the spontaneity of a loving heart she broke the jar and emptied it upon him, then and there.

Those present were shocked, then provoked. "Why such a waste?" they scolded. "That perfume could have been sold for a large sum of money and given to the poor."

Their surprises were not over. Our Lord, recovered from his initial shock and embarrassment, understood and came to her defense. "Why do you trouble the woman?" he asked. "For she has done a beautiful thing to me. For you always have the poor with you, but you will not always have me."

Then they were stunned. And so are we. So is anyone captive of arithmetic. But as they pondered what was said and done that night, a great and saving truth delivered them. Even so we may be emancipated.

First, there is deliverance from the deadly arithmetic of supposing everything must be reduced to an equation of dollars and cents.

True, some things should and must be thought of in terms of dollars and cents; but not everything, not even most things. For instance, everywhere in the world a strange phenomenon occurs: people fall in love. It is a magic made of moonbeams, stardust, tangled dreams, and tender sighs. But is it not wonderful? By its grace every woman is the fairest of the fair in some man's eyes and every man becomes Prince Charming for some lady's heart. By its bounty the cup of joy is filled to overflowing, and the landscape of everyday living lifted into beauty.

Should you walk with people on the streets of East Berlin, you would rarely hear a word spoken nor see an open, friendly face. People trudge in silence, looking straight ahead or down at their feet. Nobody smiles, nobody nods in friendly recognition. And since there is very little car traffic, all you hear is the shuffle of feet on scarred concrete. But in that place of ruins, fear, and despair I came upon two young people holding hands, looking into each other's eyes. On either side was a shambles of bomb-battered buildings. They were poorly clothed. Down the street, at intervals, men in uniform were stationed with tommy guns ready. But it mattered not to them. Something wonderful had happened: they had found each other. In this whole, wide world they had found each other! They were in love.

Just where do we put the dollar sign on that? And what happens when anyone tries to reduce it to dollars and cents?

What of home and family life that follow as ripened fruit from such goodly blossoms? Who can put a price on the healing strength that comes from knowing we are loved and trusted, even most of all by those who know our faults?

Who can hire a mother's heart to hope for us, believe in us, never lose faith in us, pray for us? Who can pay for the example of a noble and godly father?

Refrigerators, television sets, rugs, curtains, and silverware all come for a price. But they do not make a house into a home. Where would you go to buy that which makes a house a home?

And what of honor, integrity, faith, hope, courage, sympathy, understanding, wisdom, culture, salvation? Who can put them through a cash register?

Only the lowest and least in life can be reduced to dollars and cents.

Pity the man who goes through life deaf to everything but the music of a cash register. The story is told of a farmer in the Middle West who wearied of his bachelorhood and advertised: "I am thirty-eight years old. Would like to marry young woman of thirty who has tractor. Please send picture of tractor." Such a man has his reward.

Everywhere we see the shameful blight which comes from attempting to reduce life's precious perfume to the arithmetic of mere dollars and cents. Always it degrades and destroys. A man reduces honor to dollars and we have dishonesty in public office, corruption in government, bribery and "fixes" in athletics, chiseling in business—disgrace that sickens and shames us all. A woman of grace and loveliness puts a price tag upon her affection and there is the tawdry crassness of the "gold digger," the ugly decay of prostitution.

Bread and shoes, bricks and mortar, tires and gasoline; such things should and must be dealt with in the arithmetic of dollars and cents. But not everything. Not honor, love, faith, hope, courage, friendship, family affection, sympathy, prayer, dedication—not anything that is noble.

Forgetting this is surrender to death; remembering it is deliverance unto life.

Second, what happened at Bethany can deliver us from the arithmetic of the "practical."

"Why this waste? For this ointment might have been sold for a large sum, and given to the poor." Now that was being practical. But our Lord said, "No." Why?

Always he had concern for such a practical ministry to the poor. He condemned Dives, who lived in luxury while forgetting the needs of the beggar at his gate. In his parable on the Judgment he taught that devotion to him must be expressed in such practicality as feeding the hungry, clothing the naked, healing the sick; that anything less would be punished by condemnation to hell. Day after day he had lavishly given his own strength in such a ministry.

But he knew every virtue must be guarded lest it become a vice. So at Bethany Jesus was warning that even such a virtue becomes a deadly vice unless balanced by no less concern to minister unto mankind with beauty.

He was insisting that beauty is not a luxury, that mankind needs beauty even as it does bread. He was saying that devotion to him must be expressed not only in "practical" ministry to the poor, but in doing some "beautiful thing," too. "Why do you trouble the woman? For she has done a beautiful thing to me." He was asserting that the ministry of beauty must never be made to wait. "For you always have the poor with you," he reminded them. There will always be those who will need your kindly strength and care.

If beauty is a luxury, then God is a wastrel. Why should he waste himself with the making of stars and of violets, or take up space on the earth with mountains and waterfalls, or trouble himself with sunrises and butterflies?

If beauty is a luxury, then man were better a beast. Why should he struggle to make speech march in chaste and noble cadence? It is easier to grunt, even yelp. Why should he suffer as in travail to create a poem, fashion a symphony, or write a book? It is less taxing to live like sheep grazing on a hillside. Why should he trouble himself with art galleries, concerts, and architecture? It is simpler to shuffle through life like an ox.

If beauty is a luxury, let someone answer these questions. Whence comes inspiration that prompts to noble action, depth of feeling that bridges all human differences, vision that lifts eyes beyond self? Whence comes grandeur that pulls us out of pettiness and healing that makes the spirit whole? What keeps goodness from becoming sterile and love from decaying into duty? What makes the soul eager for worship and hands brave to serve? Let someone answer and say of beauty, "Why this waste?"

So, in a world of want there is reason for the precious ointment of things so impractical as an armful of roses and a skyful of stars, a *Ninth Symphony* or hills against a sunset sky, a poem or even a cathedral rising where once was a dusty parking lot.

Third, let us take a step farther and see how what was said and done at Bethany long ago has been recorded to deliver us not only from the arithmetic of the cash register and of the "practical," but also that of duty.

Obedience to duty is a noble virtue. It keeps us from shameful cowardice and weak betrayals. It saves us from slavery to whim and fancy. It gets the work of the world done. "No one who puts his hand to the plow and looks back is fit for the kingdom of God." Obedience to duty is important.

But while duty turns the necessary wheels of routine, it cannot lift us to the heights.

As Ogden Nash puts it in his "Kind of an Ode to Duty":

> O Duty,
> Why hast thou not the visage of a sweetie or a cutie?
> Why displayest thou the countenance of the kind of conscientious organizing spinster
> That the minute you see her you are aginster?
> Why glitter thy spectacles so ominously?
> Why art thou clad so abominously?
> Why art thou so different from Venus
> And why do thou and I have so few interests mutually in common between us?
> Why art thou fifty per cent. martyr
> And fifty-one per cent. Tartar?
> Why is it thy unfortunate wont
> To try to attract people by calling on them either to leave undone the deeds they like, or to do the deeds they don't?
> Why art thou so like an April post-mortem
> On something that died in the ortumn?
> Above all, why dost thou continue to hound me?
> Why art thou always albatrossly hanging around me?
> Thou so ubiquitous,

> And I so iniquitous.
> I seem to be the one person in the world thou art
>   perpetually preaching at who or to who;
> Whatever looks like fun, there art thou standing
>   between me and it, calling yoo-hoo.
> O Duty, Duty!
> How noble a man should I be hadst thou the visage
>   of a sweetie or a cutie! [1]

But when love is in the heart, then life leaps beyond the arithmetic of duty. Then the precious ointment is not measured out drop by drop. In glad devotion the jar is broken. So a little boy saves his allowance for a month and spends it to buy his mother flowers for her birthday; a young man and woman stand at an altar and pledge themselves each to the other, for better or for worse, staking their lives against any turning back. So a Schweitzer sails for Africa, a mobile medical unit leaves for Okinawa, and Christ goes out to die on a cross. So faithful Christians tithe their income and give beyond a tithe to support the work of Christ. So a people give in sacrifice to build a church.

When love is in the heart, life breaks out of the humdrum of a pitchers' duel. It fills the bases and hits the ball out of the park.

When love is in the heart, life leaps to its highest rung and though its leaping may sometimes at first appear to be a waste, always this is the greatness that saves the world.

"Why this waste? For this ointment might have been sold for a large sum, and given to the poor."

But Jesus said, "Why do you trouble the woman? For she has done a beautiful thing to me."

[1] From *I'm a Stranger Here Myself* by Ogden Nash, by permission of Little, Brown & Co. Copyright 1935, by the Curtis Publishing Co.

chapter eleven

MONOTONY—MONOTONY—
MONOTONY

THERE IS A MAN I OFTEN REMEMBER. YEARS AGO WHEN I
was a youngster employed in a gold mine I knew him. He
was a tallyman. Having lost an arm in an accident under
ground, he had been given a pension job. Day after day
underground he counted cars in trains of ore being hauled
to the hoist and dumped.

A burden of monotony pressed down upon him. At intervals throughout eight hours, trains of small mine cars
roared toward him out of dark tunnels, paused to unload,
then vanished. For eight lonely hours he merely sat and
counted cars that rattled by, all looking exactly alike;
counted them in the flickering light of his carbide lamp.

Between arrival and departure of trains and motormen
terse with haste, he sat alone in the darkness listening to
faint ticking of distant drilling machines and an occasional
series of muffled thuds from distant blasting; faraway sounds
of men busy at exciting and adventuresome jobs, work he
once had enjoyed.

Now all that remained were an empty sleeve tucked in
his jacket pocket, his solitary perch, and his regrets. There
he sat in the darkness, fifteen hundred feet underground,

tally board on his lap, counting cars hour after hour, day in and day out, through the years.

For several months I was once a motorman hauling ore out of black tunnels for him to tally. As I rode past, slowing the train to a halt, he would call out, "What, again?" "That was his greeting, invariably.

Upon changing to other work in another section of the mine, I no longer saw him underground. But frequently through the years we met on the surface coming or going from work. Always he greeted me with the same plaintive salutation, "What, again?"

He meant it in humor, of course. But looking back across the years it is evident that greeting perfectly expressed his plight. Life had become for him a train of ore cars passing by, each day like the other, dull, repetitious, an almost intolerable burden of monotony. He was caught in the drab and deadly captivity of "What, again?"

Monotony. What an aching burden!

It bears down heavily upon young men in the military services. The depressing sameness of camp life, the barrenness of the barracks, the unending chafe of feeling cooped up like a monkey in a cage. This, not the rigor and peril of active fighting, is the most difficult to endure. The slimy swamp of vice which tends to surround most any military camp thrives on monotony. Young men who haven't learned to deal wisely with boredom fall easy prey to it. Most immorality in the services grows from an attempt to escape a stifling sense of monotony.

This problem is not limited to military bases. One prime cause for juvenile delinquency anywhere is simply boredom.

Most adolescent misbehavior rises from lack of challenge, from lack of something better to do. Life is boring, so they try to brighten it up by taking over, without invitation, the home of someone away on vacation and using it for a wild party; or at 2:00 A.M. driving down a street using a sledge hammer on every parked car of one particular make. When asked, "Why did you do it?" they shrug, search for an answer, and then often reply, "Oh, it was just for kicks."

The problem is not restricted to youth. There is the woman who acts like a silly fool when she should be old enough to know better; the man at middle age who wrecks his marriage and his reputation. Usually both are revolting against monotony. There are the elderly for whom retirement has brought not release and blessing, but misery and a curse. They too are victims of monotony. And what of that miserable host, people of all ages, drearily going about, faces frozen in drooping lines of unhappiness; those for whom existence seems little better than one long, grey, smoggy day!

Who does not know what Tony the tallyman felt? Lest it destroy our defenses against temptation and rob our days of gladness, see how Jesus of Nazareth teaches mastery of monotony.

For instance, there is the familiar story of his journey through Samaria and his visit with the woman at the well near Sychar. Samaria represented monotony to Jesus. His interests were centered in Galilee, then for him a pleasant land of friendly folk where his fame already had begun to grow. But to get there, "he had to pass through Samaria." It was a long, dusty, tedious journey through an alien land where he was despised for being a Jew—for him or for any Jew a disagreeable monotony. Observe how he mastered it.

Note that he received refreshment drinking from an old well, the well of his fathers. He found succor on the long, dreary road by pausing to drink from the well many generations had found satisfying and blessed.

So we, on a forced march through some Samaria, may find refreshment. The dull drag of routine is a lonely way; monotony is an alien land with nary a friendly face. But along the way there awaits the well of our fathers, means of spiritual renewal they found satisfying and blessed.

I shall long remember a sandy-haired Scot telling of a Christmas Eve spent in a German prison camp. It was bitter cold. Their meager rations had been cut again. They had been long without mail. All of the war news was bad. The days were an unending monotony of shivering hunger, loneliness, and struggle to fight off the wolves of despair.

He was a chaplain, and as Christmas drew near, he announced a service of Holy Communion for Christmas Eve. They had no bread save the half slice allotted each man every day. As Chaplain he asked among the officers for volunteers who would save their ration of bread for the service. At the appointed hour thousands of men assembled. When he asked for the bread, four hundred officers came forward, each bearing his precious half slice of bread. So that night, he said, a campful of lonely, discouraged men celebrated the presence of Christ, gained new support from Christian fellowship, took a firm grip on God's hand, and gathered courage to go on. They were on the long, dreary journey through Samaria. But pausing at the well of their fathers, they drank deeply and found refreshment.

The church, its sacraments and its fellowship; the Bible, the practice of prayer—these are deep and ancient wells of our fathers whence floweth water, clear and refreshing, for the journey of life. Those who drink of them go forth masters of monotony.

Come farther now to see that Jesus eased the burden of monotony by drinking at "the well of another's need."

As Jesus responded to the need of the Samaritan woman, helping her find "living water," a new outlook and a new life, he likewise was refreshed and renewed. "I have meat to eat," he told his disciples, "that ye know not of." (K.J.V.)

No matter how depressing and difficult our journey through Samaria we shall often come upon "the well of another's need." There we may slake the thirst that is monotony.

If you were to nominate the greatest living woman in America, whom would you name? At the top of the list for many of us, with no one else even close, stands Helen Keller.

Imagine yourself blind, completely and forever blind. Also, suppose you are completely and forever deaf. Imagine living twenty-four hours a day in such a solitary confinement of utter darkness and total silence. Suppose you know this will be your lot to the end of life. In addition, suppose you were not only blind and deaf but that you have been dumb, that you have learned to speak only at the cost of great travail. Suppose that were your journey through Samaria!

Ever since first hearing of Helen Keller we have marveled at her accomplishments. She has broken through those obdurate walls to become a gifted writer, religious leader, public servant, champion of the oppressed. She is superior to most of us who are without her handicaps. But chiefly we have marveled at her grace and radiance of spirit, the indestructible quality of her inner strength, joy, and serenity.

How has she been able to triumph over the monotony of her journey through Samaria? What enables her to meet each new day with such zest? Part of the answer is found in letters which occasionally come bearing her carefully written signature. They are appeals urging help in behalf of the blind of the world, a cause to which she long has given lavishly of her gifts. Along the dark, dusty, dreary, silent road which is her assignment through life she pauses frequently to drink at the well of another's need. So she conquers monotony.

Are the days drab? Does dull routine dry up the springs of our gladness? Are we tired of our job, our home—perhaps even tired of our husband or our wife? Are we feeling sorry for ourselves? Are we bored, period? Then let us open our eyes and look about. On either hand are the wells of another's need. May we pause often and drink deeply. We will be surprised at how quickly monotony vanishes.

Not least, our Lord was refreshed by the well of confidence which others had in him.

Not only did the woman have confidence in him and thus find the way to new life, she ran back into the village and brought out friends and neighbors to meet him. These later said of that introduction: "we have heard for ourselves, and we know that this is indeed the Savior of the world."

Awareness of the trust others place in us is a well of refreshing, life-giving water along every weary road. It renews strength for the burdens of life. It multiplies courage to do the right. It lifts the horizons of our common days and lets the light of heaven shine through. It sets monotony to music.

Everyone is trusted by others. We trust one another as partners in a marriage, as members of a family, as members of a church, as fellow workers in our daily tasks, even when driving a car down the street. All our life is interwoven with others' lives by the golden threads of trust. Far beyond our power to comprehend, other people are trusting us, depending upon us. We are important to them.

Through sensing the faith men have in us we begin to realize the trust God places in us. He is the creator and master of the universe, but some things most important he cannot do without us. He depends upon us. Not one deed of kindness is done unless we do it for him. Not one step is taken in leading mankind into his kingdom—the kingdom of justice, mercy, wisdom, beauty, holiness, and peace—unless we take it for him. As the old familiar poem wisely puts it:

> Christ has no hands but our hands
> To do His work today,

> He has no feet but our feet
> To lead men in His way,
> He has no tongue but our tongues
> To tell men how He died,
> He has no help but our help
> To bring them to His side.[1]

Close beside the road on every journey through dry and alien Samaria is the well of awareness that others, even God, are trusting us. It brings refreshment and renewal that conquers monotony.

Well, here's the answer to Tony the tallyman.

When we must travel through Samaria, that land of dull routine and dreary monotony, the Lord of life walks at our side. He points to wells along the way which yield life-changing refreshment to all who drink from them.

---

[1] Annie Johnson Flint, "The World's Bible." Copyright. Reproduced by permission. Evangelical Publishers, Toronto, Canada.

chapter twelve

COME RAIN OR
COME SHINE

A MAN IS UNDER ARREST AND THREAT OF DEATH. EVIDENTLY
he has been imprisoned for some time. His trial, long
delayed, is in but its preliminary stages. Despite pretense
of law and due process, he is subject to the fickle and depraved whim of a dictator. From hour to hour he lives
suspended by a thread over any fate.

Friends faraway, learning of his plight, raise a purse and
send one of their number to help in every way possible.
In response, he sends back a letter, one of the most intimate and beautiful which come to us from the ancient
world. Toward its close he says to these anxious friends,
don't worry about me, "I have learned to be content, whatever the circumstances may be. I know now how to live
when things are difficult and I know how to live when
things are prosperous. In general and in particular I have
learned the secret of facing either poverty or plenty. I am
ready for anything through the strength of the one who
lives within me." (Phil. 4:11-13 Phillips.)

I have learned the secret, the apostle Paul says, of being
content, "come rain or come shine." Who is not in need
of that wisdom for life?

Contentment! That is a peaceable word. But it gets a preacher into trouble. Let him advocate contentment and immediately he is misunderstood.

Followers of Karl Marx say, "Ah, there you have admitted it. Christianity is an opiate. It makes people complacent, docile, submissive; robbing them of inner fire and determination to stand up against injustice and oppression. It is a drug used by the rich and mighty to exploit the poor and the weak."

More numerous and dangerous than Communist critics, however, are they who, in search of contentment, rush off to the other extreme. They would reduce Christianity to the level of soothing syrup, tranquilizers, and bromo-seltzer and believe they have done themselves and mankind a great service. They think of God as a glorified masseur and imagine themselves very pious.

But this is not the contentment Paul advocated. He was not complacent, docile, and submissive. Christianity was for him a spur, not a drug. It prompted him to toil and suffer for the birth of a new humanity. He was charged with turning the world upside down. When thrown into prison, he continued in the service of Christ, making converts of his guards and even a jailer, transforming faint-hearted visitors into bold evangels of the faith, writing letters of wisdom and encouragement to Christians across the known world, some of which today we read in the New Testament. Obviously, his was not the contentment Communists hold up to ridicule and others use as a righteous excuse for pampering and indulging self. He made a creative use of contentment.

This is Christian contentment, and we need it. Like

Paul, we dare not be content with evil within ourselves or in the world outside ourselves, nor put the concerns of self above our duty in the service of Christ. But we do need a contentment which prevents waste of energy in chafing resentment and blind fighting, guards against self-pity and craven despair, and girds us to play the man, whatever life brings. We need contentment which creates within a citadel of quietness, wise acceptance, and brave endurance; which makes for steadiness and assurance, zest for living, and a song—"come rain or come shine."

Where and how do we find it?

According to Paul, we begin to make life an adventure in creative contentment by appreciating what we have rather than lamenting what we lack.

Although a prisoner in Rome, subject to the caprice of a dictator so depraved he delighted in witnessing human torture and death, Paul could write: "I have learned to be content, whatever the circumstances. . . . I know now how to live when things are difficult."

Despite humiliation, frustration, loneliness, and every other unpleasant aspect of that situation, he won contentment through thankfulness. He rejoiced in friends who remained loyal and in the opportunity provided by his chains to make converts even among the palace guards. He was grateful that faltering Christians found new courage in his willingness to be a prisoner for Christ and that sharing in the suffering of Christ made for growth in the likeness of Christ. Celebrating good memories of work accomplished, he gave thanks that in Christ were resources which made his spirit glad and free, the master of circumstance.

115

He did not lament what he lacked. He rejoiced in what he had. So he was content.

A clipping dating back to the days of World War II shows a scene in a town of northwestern England after a bombing raid. In the background can be seen what a few hours previously had been a home. In the foreground is a group of people in various attire standing about a piano in the middle of the street. The piano, scratched and battered, together with a few chairs and knicknacks, evidently is all that remained for that family. But the picture shows them singing.

It was partly bravado and good propaganda, of course. But it was more than that. They were thankful for what remained. Having lost a house, they were grateful that they had not lost their lives, nor their love for one another, nor laughter, nor music, nor the stars at night, nor the loveliness of their countryside, nor their faith in God. Rather than complain over what they had lost, they rejoiced in what they still had.

This is one rewarding step toward possessing a creative contentment. No matter what may happen, even the worst of calamity and sorrow, there always remains something for which to be thankful, blessings that can make music in the heart "come rain or come shine."

Also, we learn from Paul that genuine contentment is found through building upon what we have. Given leisure, he used it for study, prayer, and the writing of letters. Given chains, he used them to glorify his Lord. Given hardships, disappointments, and peril of death, he used them to tighten his grip upon God. He built upon what he had. So, he was content, "come rain or come shine."

Some years ago a brilliant young physician, after establishing a lucrative practice in London's West End, became seriously ill. It looked like the end of the road—at least the end of his success as a doctor.

In hope of recovery, he went to the Highlands of Scotland. There he lived with a dour but friendly farmer and wife in a lonely, whitewashed cottage set beside a rain-drenched lake. Round about were ferocious mountains rearing jagged peaks into grey mist.

At first he was nearly beside himself with loneliness and disappointment. Finally, he took stock of what remained and decided to build upon it. He recalled that years before he had cherished a desire to write. He had leisure and a fragment of strength. So, he went to the nearby village, bought two dozen penny tablets, came home, went up to his clean, cold bedroom with its scrubbed table and hard chair, sat down, and began to write. It was difficult and painful, especially at first. But the old farmer with his inborn Scottish reverence for "letters" encouraged him and he continued. Slowly, in much travail, he built upon what he had. Finally, from that cold, clean bedroom on a lonely farm beside a rain-drenched lake amid mountains clothed in mist, a book went forth. It was translated into nineteen languages and made into a movie.

A. J. Cronin was a man who thought he had lost everything. Then on second thought he took stock of what remained and built upon it. That was the beginning for one of our generation's most gifted novelists.

We are disappointed? We have lost what we dearly cherished? We think life has been unfair to us? Then why not turn from mourning what we have lost or the evil that has befallen us and take an inventory of what we have? We will be surprised what God can help us build upon it!

We come now to the heart of Christian contentment: trust in God. Above all else Paul trusted God. This was his fountain of contentment, a clear, bubbling, sparkling spring of strength, courage, peace, and joy.

Trusting God, he was content in knowing his treasure was secure. He trusted God enough to lay up his treasure in heaven. He invested his life in the service of truth and righteousness, in self-forgetting ministry for others, in the nurture and growth of Christian personality and character, in the adventure of an unfolding life with God through Christ. This was treasure nothing could destroy: neither mobs, nor scourging, nor jails, nor sickness, nor pain, nor shipwrecks, nor Nero, nor death. It was a treasure, to use words of Jesus, "where neither moth nor rust doth corrupt, and where thieves do not break through nor steal." (K.J.V.) He was Christ's, and Christ was God's. Nothing could separate him from his treasure. He was content "come rain or come shine."

How much misery we bring upon ourselves when, unlike Paul, we put our trust not in God but in things of earth. We forget that what is of the earth is subject to every attrition of the earth and is fickle as the clouds. Money slips from dying fingers, health fails under the weight of years, a home too soon becomes a place of aching silences, friends and loved ones disappear down the road from which none return. All things of earth are transient as the wind. We have them today, but who knows what the morrow will bring? Sooner than we think, all will be gone.

To anchor our heart in treasures of earth is to play the rich fool. All too soon the day of darkness overtakes us and nothing remains, nought but ashes and anguish. The wise among us trust in God enough to invest themselves in treasure of heaven. This does not fade and fail. It is treasure which grows richer with the years. Increasingly it blesses the earth and rejoices their heart. They look upon it and are content.

Better still, trusting in God, Paul knew he was adequate for anything. "I have learned to be content, whatever the circumstances." Why? He follows quickly with the answer: "I am ready for anything through the strength of the one who lives within me." He trusted God enough to make God's will his will. Living in harmony with God, God's presence and power indwelled in him. Thus he was equipped to be the master of circumstance.

The future is an unknown road. We never know what lion may suddenly appear and bar the way for us. But this we do know: there will be lions. Again and again we shall meet disappointment, trouble, sorrow, calamity. Of such is our human lot. But like Paul, trusting in the God we know through Jesus Christ, we can be "ready for anything."

> God is my strong salvation:
>   What foe have I to fear?
> In darkness and temptation,
>   My light, my help, is near:
> Though hosts encamp around me,
>   Firm in the fight I stand;

What terror can confound me,
　　With God at my right hand?

Place on the Lord reliance;
　　My soul, with courage wait;
His truth be thine affiance,
　　When faint and desolate;
His might thy heart shall strengthen,
　　His love thy joy increase;
Mercy thy days shall lengthen;
　　The Lord will give thee peace.

To know this—more, to believe and practice it—is to be content "come rain or come shine."

chapter thirteen

THE BIBLE CAN
BE READ

SOME TIME AGO A MAN TALKED WITH ME ABOUT THE BIBLE. "Last winter," he said, "I resolved to read the Bible, to read it thoroughly. My mother and a godly Sunday-school teacher taught me, when I was a boy, that the Bible is a holy book; that through its pages God speaks; that I should read it devoutly and thoughtfully every day. If I did this, they assured me, the Bible would be an unfailing source of divine wisdom and strength, comfort and peace.

"I long believed all of this, but never did anything about it until a year ago. I knew I needed the help they told me the Bible would give. Even if that had not been the case, I thought it was high time for me, a literate person, to get a firsthand acquaintance with the 'world's greatest book.'

"So I got a Bible and started in. For more than a week I spent an hour every evening before going to bed reading the Bible. My wife was amazed. But I got in the middle of all that business about Moses and the wilderness and never got out. It was too much for me."

Then with much earnestness he concluded: "I know I ought to read the Bible. I feel guilty because I don't. I wish you could tell me how to read it so I could get some good out of it."

If the truth were known, he is legion. Not many of us are at peace with what we do concerning the Bible. We have been taught certain great affirmations about the Bible. These we want to believe, if for no reason than loyalty to those we love and respect. But in the light of our knowledge we wonder how we can, and at the same time be intellectually honest. We have been taught certain practices regarding use of the Bible. But upon beginning we bog down in mental conflict, bewilderment, or boredom.

Apart from the practice of prayer, what is there of hallowed status and holy purpose about which more people, good people, have such deep misgiving, chafing confusion, and uneasy turns of conscience! The Bible, for many instead of giving light and strength, peace and gladness, is cause for perplexity and a pursuing sense of guilt.

See how the Bible can be what it was for our fathers: the Book of books; the wisdom, strength, joy, and peace of God for our daily lives; the way of salvation; our greatest help and dearest treasure. How can we "give the Bible a chance"?

Certainly one requirement is this: Start where beginners can have success.

If we have never ridden a horse we should not begin on a high-spirited colt or an irascible veteran with psychotic tendencies lest our ambitions humiliate, betray, and defeat us. One minute, yea verily ten seconds, on a horse too much for us to ride can make us forever wish we had never seen one. If we and those with whom we trust our fate on

122

such an occasion have so much as a smidgen of horse sense, we begin with some staid, philosophical old dobbin who long ago decided that the best way through life is to endure quietly the eccentricities of strange bipeds who insist upon climbing upon his back.

My friend, whose resolve to read the Bible perished in the wilderness with Moses and the children of Israel, made the mistake of beginning where it is difficult for a beginner to win success: He started with too much horse.

This is a common error. People assume the Bible, like any other book, is best read by starting at page one and proceeding page by page until the end is reached. The Bible, however—in this particular especially—is not like other books.

It is not one book; it is a library of books bound for convenience and common purpose between two covers. It contains books of history, poetry, biography, romance, essays, sermons—sixty-six all told. These books were written by scores of writers over a period of more than one thousand years. Some of them reach back to the dimmest beginnings of the human story, back to the myths and folk legends by which primitive man preserved and conveyed his history long before there was a written language. Taken together, these sixty-six books reveal a panorama of cultural change ranging from the primitivism of stone-age man and the first dawn of civilization to the sophistication of the Greco-Roman world at its prime. They span the rise and fall of nations, the beginning and end of empires, the birth and death of civilizations. They constitute a library in which, as nowhere else, we view the human scene and touch the throbbing heart of all mankind.

123

The sequence by which these sixty-six books have been arranged serves a purpose, of course; but that purpose is not the convenience of beginners. Hence, instead of starting our adventure with the Bible at page one, chapter one, book one, we should begin at a place more acceptable to our understanding and relevant to our experience. We should start with a horse we can ride.

For instance, should our resolution to read the Bible coincide with the season of Christmas, it would be most appropriate to start with the Gospel of Luke and its beautiful story of Bethlehem and the Babe. Upon completing that Gospel, we could go to the other three Gospels. When we have completed them, we could turn to the history of the early church as recorded in Acts. From thence we might proceed to the Psalms, the poetry of Israel; then to the letters of Paul, the writings of the prophets and the wisdom literature of the Old Testament, not forgetting the Book of Job and its superb drama dealing with the problem of evil and suffering. Last, perhaps, we could embark upon the early history of Israel as found in the opening books of the Bible.

To give the Bible a chance, start where beginners most easily can win success. Begin with a horse you can ride.

In addition to beginning sensibly, use aids which are available for understanding the Bible. Attendance in a church-school class or a midweek meeting where a trained leader has opportunity to teach can be of continual assistance. Invaluable aid can be found through use of a few good books such as a one-volume Bible commentary which can be bought for less than a year's subscription to a daily paper and will last a lifetime. A Bible dictionary would also be helpful. Such books make available to us the best of scholarship and can be used by anyone with great profit who has so much as an eighth-grade education.

The Bible is the product and the object of more painstaking scholarship and sacrificial toil by more dedicated people across the centuries than any other book ever written. It is entitled, therefore, as is no other book, to thoughtful use of aids to understanding which able minds and rich experience put at our disposal.

It is important also to remember that the Bible did not drop from heaven ready-made—finished, signed, sealed, and delivered. As the story of Christmas reminds us, God does not bestow his blessings upon mankind in that way. Just as the gift of his Son came by way of lowly birth and the flesh of our frailty, so came the Bible. It was born of heaven and of earth, of God and of man. It is the product of a partnership between God and man. In that partnership God did not reduce man to a teletype machine, writing what he did not comprehend. God never reduces man to an automaton, however quicker and easier that might be for him to speak his word and have his will obeyed. Dictators work that way, not God.

What God values most is the integrity of an individual, his need and right to think and choose in freedom. So in creating the Bible God took the long, slow way of working with and through each writer's mind and personality. Each was trusted to think and express his thoughts in freedom. That method is slow. It admits much error. But it is the only way by which his truth can emerge and be transmitted.

For this reason we find such a difference between the

various books of the Bible. Each writer was free to be himself—free to reflect his own temperament and religious experience, his own interpretation of world events and culture, his own theology and knowledge of physical sciences.

Hence, we meet contradictory statements in the Bible, some of which violate common knowledge and Christian ethics. Jesus, for example, found it necessary to correct certain teaching in the Old Testament, saying:

> Ye have heard that it hath been said, An eye for an eye, and a tooth for a tooth: But I say unto you, That ye resist not evil: but whosoever shall smite thee on thy right cheek, turn to him the other also. . . . Ye have heard that it has been said, Thou shalt love thy neighbour, and hate thine enemy. But I say unto you, Love your enemies, bless them that curse you.
>
> (K.J.V.)

The Bible has in it the grain of God and the straw of man. It is heaven-inspired, but earth-made.

Another imperative is integrity. The Bible is an honest book. It is entitled to honest treatment. This means we must never attempt to force the Bible into a purpose for which it was not written.

We should not expect the Bible to serve as a textbook on science, for instance; nor should we resort to mental gymnastics in attempting to prove that it does. The writers of the Bible, being free to express awareness of truth through the alembic of their own understanding, naturally reflected the science of their times.

For example, as late as A.D. 600 learned men believed that the earth was flat, four hundred days' journey long, two hundred days' journey wide, and that it was surrounded by seas. This seemed to be a reasonable explanation of apparent facts. After all, from the facts known to them didn't the earth look flat? Besides, how could human beings keep from falling off if it were not flat? Furthermore, who could travel by land more than a hundred days and not arrive at an ocean whose waters stretched forth into infinity?

In ancient times learned men believed the sky was supported by pillars which surrounded the distant rim of the earth and its surrounding seas. That seemed sensible. How else, they asked, could the blue dome of the sky with the stars, the moon, and the sun be held in place above the earth?

They assumed that the flat earth and its heavenly dome were sandwiched between great bodies of water. That appeared most reasonable. After all, when you dug down into the earth you came upon water, and most evidently rain came down from above. So when it rained, they said, "the heavens opened."

They believed devils and demons of various kinds infested the air like flies. Did a man suffer severe pain in the region of his stomach? He had a demon in there. Did it hurt like the very mischief? Most probably many demons had come uninvited and taken up residence. What would bring health? Their answer was simple: Persuade, bribe, frighten, or in any other way get the demons out. To this day among primitive people a cure for sickness is attempted by thrusting needles into the sufferer's body where pain is most intense, thereby providing the demons with an avenue of escape or making them so uncomfortable they will find their own means of exit. Was a woman given to violent rage? Did she tongue-lash unfortunate victims who got in her way? She had a demon, they believed, perhaps many demons. The remedy? Get rid of the demons.

Such was the science of the ancient world. We find it in the Bible as in all other literature of those times. It seems quaint to us, but to them it was most sensible, even as two thousand years from now science which to us seems sensible will seem most quaint. Of this, however, we can be certain: The Bible as a source of spiritual insight and Christian motivation will have as much authority two thousand years hence as it did then and as it does now.

The Bible was created not to provide the latest facts and theories of science but to serve souls of men—to teach them what God is and what man can become; to turn men from the destruction of error and sin; to lead men into the resources which build them up in wisdom, goodness, love, and usefulness to their fellows. The supreme purpose of the Bible is to bring men to a saving knowledge of God and to establish them in the way of life revealed best by Jesus Christ. For this purpose the Bible was created. For this purpose honesty directs its use.

Also, to give the Bible a hearing, do not allow lack of understanding to be a roadblock. Proceed to use and apply what you can understand.

Most everything we use in life reaches beyond our understanding. We don't understand the miracle of birth, but we proceed to build homes and rear children. We don't understand the miracle of sight, but we proceed to use our eyes regularly. We don't understand the miracle by which oxygen, hydrogen, carbon dioxide, and carbon are maintained in the proper amount and relationship required for the existence of life upon this planet, but we proceed daily with the business of living.

Even so, though we may not understand all of the Bible, or even most of it, we can understand enough to use it daily to our great profit. As somebody has said, the Bible is like the ocean—a child can play in it, an elephant can swim in it.

Gradually, as we continue to read the Bible regularly, thoughtfully, and devoutly, and as our experience deepens and knowledge increases, more and more of the Bible will stand open and luminous before us. But of this we can be sure: The Bible will be a challenge to our mind so long as we live. We will never outgrow it.

Supremely, we must read the Bible devoutly and expectantly. It is a holy book. Through the generations men have found as in no other book on earth awareness of God's presence; and they have heard him speaking to them personally. Hence, when reading the Bible we can be sure he is at our sides, closer than breathing, nearer than hands and feet. Always we should listen for what he is saying. As someone has said: "When He condemns, bow penitently. When He offers help, place your hope on that assurance. When He commands, obey. When He guides, follow."

By every standard of measurement, the Bible is the world's greatest book. By every means of discernment it is evident that we, as individuals and as a generation, need what the Bible can do for and through us.

chapter fourteen

IF A MAN DIE

"If a man die, shall he live again?" that is an old, old question but always it is being brought up to date.

Several years ago I stood with a couple at an altar when, with radiant faces, they exchanged vows of marriage. They were young and gloriously in love. Life stretched out before them rich with promise. Recently a letter came from the bride of that day. With permission, I share these excerpts:

My husband and I had over three years of the most wonderful marriage possible. On Labor Day last he was terribly burned while fighting a forest fire. . . . He died as a result of his burns. . . . We all believed he would get well, though he suffered greatly. His lungs, however, were seared too badly.

Since then many questions have been jumbled up in my mind. I want so much to see him again some day. I am so eager for help and assurance. . . . Do you know of any material in addition to the Bible which I could read that might be of help? . . .

Five weeks after he was called to be with God, I received a most wonderful gift—a baby girl. When I look at that sweet little face that looks so much like him, I feel very grateful and wonder how I can have any doubts. . . . Yet each day brings dark thoughts and many moments of wondering. . . . He was such a fine Christian boy, surely all of those good traits cannot be stopped by death.

They were young, gloriously in love, and their dreams were coming true. Today she is a widow and, in the dark night of loneliness, is reaching out a hand for reassurance. "If a man dies, shall he live again?" For her the old question is as ever present as her heartbeats.

When young, this rarely disturbs us. Death is something that happens only to other people. We dream, plan, go about the business of living as if we were to be here forever. Nor do we think of death as invading our family or circle of friends. Death is always something peculiar and foreboding involving only other people.

But as we grow more mature, this make-believe world in which death never enters loses its power to blind and bewitch us. Gradually, sometimes with catastrophic swiftness, our childish illusions collapse and we face the shattering truth. We see time's ruin and know it for the great destroyer. "Change and decay in all around [we] see." We hear the inexorable beat of death's oncoming feet, coming for us and all dear to us. Then, gone our world of fantasy. We know that on earth, for everything and everyone, death is king. So, the old question becomes *the* question: "If a man die, shall he live again?"

What is the answer? If we look no deeper than sight and sound, no farther than the reach of our senses, if we limit reality to what can be weighed and measured, then of course the answer is no. Death is king, now and forever. Then we must say with Bertrand Russell, "Brief and powerless is man's life; on him and all his race the slow sure doom falls, pitiless and dark."

But the Christian faith gives another answer. It speaks for dimensions of reality which admit the fact of the supernatural, which provide foundations for belief in life everlasting, even such an affirmation as:

"Our Savior Christ Jesus, who abolished death and brought life and immortality to light through the gospel." Believing this, we can look death full in the face and put it in its proper place, viewing it as an incident rather than a tyrant. We can say with John Donne:

> Death, be not proud, though some have called thee
> Mighty and dreadful, for thou art not so;
> For those whom thou think'st thou dost overthrow
> Die not, poor Death, nor yet canst thou kill me.

Consider now several honest reasons which support such a conviction.

There is knowledge that reality does exceed the reach of our physical senses.

During the past two centuries, of course, there has been strong opinion in certain quarters to the contrary. While modern science was in its first full bloom it was commonplace in some circles to assume the universe is a product of chance and ruled by blind force—a vast machine grinding its way in the blind circle of cause and effect, quite without meaning and purpose, impervious to every human hope, deaf to every human cry. Man was conceived an animal, a machine, a captive of his glands, a creature of circumstance, a biological-chemical combination of body and brain—that much and no more.

In such a view of the universe and of man there is, of course, neither room nor reason for the existence of God. Neither is there possibility for man to have a soul, moral freedom, and hope of immortality. August Comte, materialist-philosopher of the past century, voiced this viewpoint when he bid farewell to God, saying: "When science has done its complete work, it will conduct God to the boundary of the universe and bow him out with thanks for his provisional services."

But leave it to the Russians to win the prize! Recently several Russian Communist scientists gave the ultimate expression to this viewpoint, when in a news release from Moscow they stated that recent probing of interplanetary space thoroughly disproved the existence of God, immortality, and heaven. In all the information sent back by the sputniks and by man-in-space, said they, there was no evidence of an encounter with God or angels, nor evidence of a place where dwell immortal souls departed from the earth.

At first I thought this was a new form of Communist humor. But it was not. They were playing it straight, to their viewpoint. This, they thought, was evidence to support the official Communist repudiation of religion. As if, to be real, God and the hosts of heaven should be physical objects riding about on a space platform somewhere between here and Venus!

This folly of restricting reality to sense data, however, has largely passed. Most thoughtful people now share the conviction that there is much more to reality than things which can be measured by science, even discovered by sputniks and astronauts. They appreciate science as a highly developed and valuable technique for working with the quantitative aspect of our experience; the subhuman, mathematical, mechanical strata of reality. But they insist there is a qualitative level of reality which is the realm of consciousness, personality, and ideas—reality which is the domain of the soul. This, they point out, is quite beyond the range and competence of science for the simple reason that we cannot weigh an idea, isolate consciousness in a test tube, or dissect a hope. This, the qualitative level of reality, they insist, is what is most important for human beings.

They believe that the universe, in so far as it is mechanical, does have a Master who rules it creatively, not violating its orderliness; One who makes its laws responsive to his intelligent will, moral purpose, and loving concern for the sons of men, his children.

They believe the universe and its Sovereign respond to and support human values; that man is not a victim or a product to be predicted and controlled, but a living soul of free moral choice; that man is more than animal and machine, more than can be weighed and measured by scientific devices; that he has such spiritual qualities as consciousness and self-awareness, capacity for conscience and self-criticism, concern for purpose and awareness of the Holy; that such qualities are the most important attributes of man. In short, they believe man has a soul as well as a body.

Knowledge that reality is bigger than the measure of our physical senses gives solid support to belief in life eternal.

Also, belief in life eternal is supported by knowledge

which arises from our personal experience and intuition, knowledge which is indigenous to all mankind.

As life progresses, we become dissatisfied with anything less than immortality. As Baron von Hugel once described it: "We have the salt [of eternity] on our lips." When we are young, with death seeming so alien that it is merely an academic interest, we may find it easy to spurn concern for immortality as, for example, did Thomas Huxley, in a letter to John Morley, once wrote: "It is a curious thing that I find my dislike to the thought of extinction increasing as I get older and nearer the goal. . . . I had sooner be in hell a good deal—at any rate in one of the upper circles, where the climate and the company are not too trying."

This is more than mere selfish interest to survive. It is grounded upon awareness that our highest concerns and capacities demand the dimensions of eternity. Victor Hugo, when an old man, had this to say:

I feel in myself the future life. I am like a forest once cut down; the new shoots are stronger and livelier than ever. I am rising, I know, toward the sky. The sunshine is on my head. The earth gives me its generous sap, but heaven lights me with the reflection of unknown worlds.

You say the soul is nothing but the resultant of the bodily powers? Why, then, is my soul more luminous when my body powers begin to fail? Winter is on my head, but eternal spring is in my heart . . . The nearer I approach the end, the plainer I hear around me the immortal symphonies of the worlds which invite me. It is marvelous yet simple. . . .

For half a century I have been writing my thoughts in prose and in verse; history, philosophy, drama, romance, tradition, satire, ode and song; I have tried all. But I feel I have not said the thousandth part of what is in me. When I go down to the grave I can say like many others, "I have finished my day's work." But I cannot say, "I have finished my life." My day's work will begin again the next morning. The tomb is not a blind alley; it is a thoroughfare. It closes on the twilight. It opens on the dawn.[1]

But there is yet a deeper reason for our unwillingness to accept the finality of death. This is our rebellion against belief that someone dear to us, dearer than our own life, should be obliterated by death, cast off as if of no value. On occasion we may accept the thought of the total annihilation of ourselves as not incredible, even as desirable. But who can thus accept death for someone he loves? Ernest Hocking of Harvard tells of a letter from an old friend, for years a hardheaded skeptic and naturalist, who had lost his dearly loved wife. He wrote:

I have never taken any stock in the notion of anyone living after death. It is too contrary to everything that we biologists seem to see with our eyes. But when [she] died, I suddenly realized that as biologists we see nothing that touches the question at all. We see the body die, and we think of life as a property of the body. But consciousness and personality we do not see; they are not the same as organic life. I have a feeling deeper than any argument, nor affected by argument, that she cannot have vanished from the universe.[2]

[1] As quoted in Albert W. Palmer, Aids to Worship (New York: The Macmillan Company, 1944), pp. 65-66.

[2] From Man's Destiny in Eternity (Boston: Beacon Press, 1949), p. 161. Reprinted by permission of the Beacon Press, copyright 1949 by F. Lyman Windolph and Farmers' Bank & Trust Company of Lancaster.

No one can long evade or convincingly deny the reasons for belief in life eternal which arise out of the experience and intuition of the race, even our own.

> Just when we are safest, there's a sunset-touch,
> A fancy from a flower-bell, some one's death,
> A chorus-ending from Euripides,
> And that's enough for fifty hopes and fears
> As old and new at once as Nature's self,
> To rap and knock and enter in our soul.
> —ROBERT BROWNING, *Bishop Blougram's Apology*

But, of course, for Christians the strongest reason for faith in life eternal is found in the Easter shout: "He is risen." That to us is evidence indubitable of certain, great, decisive, and redemptive facts, facts as basic as creation itself.

Here is a witness to the fact of the supernatural. It tells us that God is more than a vague abstraction for the convenience of philosophy, that he is not a prisoner of his own creation, shackled by his own laws. It declares he is a loving Father, ever present to sustain and succor his children, free to direct nature for man's good. It says, "Believe in the rationality of interpreting the universe in terms of its best; believe that in the life and deeds, death and resurrection of Jesus Christ we see best of all what God is and does." It says, "Believe there is a greatness about us, beyond us, above us; a greatness purposive and redemptive, free to work creatively in and with us."

It is a witness to the infinite worth of persons. The gospel declares to us and every man: "Christ died on the cross for you. That is your value. You are more precious in God's sight than a million stars. Death does not make you a discard. God will not cast you off merely because your body wears out; rather, he would draw you closer to him. Death is not the end of the journey for you. It is only a turn in the road which brings you closer to the greatness of God. The stuff of eternity is in you. You are made in his image, made to be with him forever and ever!"

Here is the answer to that young wife and mother, so recently made a widow. Here is the conquering answer to the old question, ever new. With this we are set free to put death in its proper place, released to live with hope and joy.

chapter fifteen

TRUST IN GOD?

Trust in god? why should we? how can we?

It is time-honored advice. Most of us were reared upon it. It is as indigenous to American heritage and custom as the Fourth of July.

We meet it in presidential proclamations and other official documents. We find it inscribed upon our currency; that is, the small change up to and including one dollar bills. For some reason, "In God We Trust," has never reached the more serious money. Despite the omission, we wish to be known as a people who trust in God.

That belief has substantial foundations. We are political descendants of the Mayflower Pact, the Declaration of Independence, and the Constitution of the United States. They are the oft-avowed fruits of trust in God. We are cultural descendants of the Greeks who, while exalting man to new status, defined him as a creature who looks above and beyond himself in awareness of and trust in the Divine. They called man *anthropos*, which means "the upward-looking one." We are spiritual descendants of people who wrote the Bible, the most eloquent witness for trust in God. Our line reaches back to those who sang as they climbed the stony, dusty roads to Jerusalem:

> I will lift up my eyes to the hills.
> From whence does my help come?
> My help comes from the Lord,
>   who made heaven and earth.

Politically, culturally, and religiously we have been cradled in that stalwart affirmation of mind, heart and soul: trust in God. Further, as we take the measure of our interior resources in these brittle, frenetic times, we know how great our need for this faith of our fathers.

But trust in God, like every other spiritual treasure of our heritage, must be won anew by each successive generation. We may inherit its traditions, vocabulary, and institutions. We may even sense our present need of it. But it and its fruits quickly become of no more value than a museum piece unless it finds renewed life in our lives; unless we too, in basic attitude, commitment, and practice, trust in God.

One essential for the birth and nurture of such faith is the conviction that there is a God who cares.

What is the ultimate Fact, that from which all else derives; or, as C. S. Lewis has described it, "the thing you can't go behind"? What is the source and animating power of all creation?

Some take rocks, atoms, and electrons as the clue. They interpret reality in terms of blind force. That which appears as order and beauty is the product of a cosmic accident. Man himself is a cosmic joke. The universe, born of chance and sustained by irrational, impersonal energy, is a vast machine grinding its way through measureless space and infinite time, impervious to every human hope, deaf to every human cry.

If that be a true and sensible interpretation of Reality, then Mencken was right when he said man's existence can be likened to that of a sick fly taking a dizzy ride on a gigantic flywheel of cause and effect; then James B. Cabell was right when he declared man was no more than "a bundle of cellular material on its way to becoming manure." Then, of course, the faith of our fathers known as "trust in God" is sheer nonsense.

But all great religion stands on the assumption that the human, not the subhuman; the personal, not the impersonal, should be our clue for interpreting reality.

Should man himself be interpreted merely in terms of the size of his shoes, the color of his skin, the functioning of his digestive system, or his golf handicap? No, we say. In fairness to truth he should be understood in terms of his most significant qualities and achievements. We must take into account the nature of his personality, the level of his character, the quality of his mind. We must scale his dimensions to include the causes he serves, the beauty he creates, the wisdom he gains, the love he gives, the prayers he offers. We believe the full truth is not told about man until it includes the highest of which he is capable.

For this very reason, religion takes its stand against atheism. It says the full truth is not told about the Creator until it includes the highest of which we know he is capable. Religion insists that in fairness to truth the Creator should be understood not merely in terms of unthinking stones or irrational, amoral nuclear energy, but also in terms of personality: human beings capable of thought, decision, freedom, creative endeavor, moral growth, spiritual discernment, sacrificial love, and fellowship, both human and divine. Religion refutes the dreary pettiness and blindness of the godless with the insistence that the Creator is best revealed by his highest creation, which is persons.

We Christians go from there to affirm God is best revealed by the noblest of all persons, Jesus Christ. We say God is at least as much as was the historic Jesus, that in his words we hear God speak, in his deeds of compassion we see what God does, in his death we know the measure of God's love for us, in his resurrection we are assured of God's triumph over sin and death, a victory open to us through him.

On such ground of fact and reason we lay claim to the faith of our fathers, to trust in God.

We affirm there is a God who cares. We believe that beyond matter is mind, beyond multiplicity is purpose, beyond power is a personal Being, beyond the prison of cause and effect is redemptive love—with a key. The universe is not empty of meaning; God is there. It does not mock our deepest yearnings and highest desires; God is there. Someone is in charge whose wisdom is omniscient, whose power is omnipotent, whose righteousness is absolute, whose justice is perfect, whose mercy is unfailing, whose name is Love! There is a God who cares.

We believe for good reason that the fundamental truth about the nature of things is this: There is a God whose face we see in Jesus Christ, a God who cares. Standing on this foundation, we trust in God.

What derives from trusting in God? Values beyond price.

Therein is motivation for doing one's best in midst of the worst. Just six years ago a village church in England celebrated its three hundredth anniversary. On a wall of that church is this inscription: "In the year 1653, when all things sacred were throughout the nation either demolished or profaned, Sir Robert Shirley, Baronet, founded this church; whose singular praise it is to have done the best things in the worst times and hoped them in the most calamitous." Sir Robert Shirley trusted in God. Therein he found incentive to do the best in midst of the worst.

We remember Jesus of Nazareth in the Garden of Gethsemane. The traitor already had gone for his thirty pieces of silver. Soon Judas would be leading the soldiers through the night and across the valley to that quiet place of loveliness, there to seize our Lord like a common criminal.

He yet had time to escape. Under cover of night he could flee to the wilderness and by dawn be safe. He could hide for a few months until the furor had quieted and then resume private life far to the north. He could live out his life like other men.

Jesus was young. The love of life was strong in him. He knew what would follow arrest: a mock trial, humiliation, torture, and finally crucifixion. Already he could feel the nails and the mocking stare of the crowd. He cringed under it, shrank from it. All that was human in him cried out to escape it.

Most of his friends had fled. Those who remained would gladly flee with him.

Time was running out. What should he do? In agony

he prayed: "My Father, if it be possible, let this cup pass from me; nevertheless, not as I will, but as thou wilt." Thus, he won the victory. He was able to rise and meet the traitor and the soldiers and so go to his cross the strong Son of God. He trusted in God. So, in the midst of the worst he could serve the best.

Trace the origin of every movement for social reform, every bold forward thrust in the cause of truth and justice, freedom and righteousness; of every institution which now blesses our common life with the privileges of democracy, opportunities of education, and the skylines of great religion. All is the harvest of those who in midst of the worst found incentive to serve the best through trust in God.

How much we need such incentive!

Also, through trust in God we can make a creative use of trouble. This is what Paul meant when out of hardship and persecution he wrote: "We rejoice in our sufferings, knowing that suffering produces endurance, and endurance produces character and character produces hope, and hope does not disappoint us, because God's love has been poured into our hearts."

Should we fail to make such a use of trouble, life would become too much for us. Fear and despair would rule the day.

One of the prize stories about Martin Luther tells of a time when his troubles had all but crushed him. Usually stalwart and indomitable, he went about cloaked in despair. After he had gone his gloomy way for some weeks, becoming increasingly pessimistic and short tempered, his wife thought of a remedy. She presented herself in the domain of his study dressed in mourning, weeping bitterly. Luther was stunned. "What tragedy has befallen us now?" he wondered. "Katie," he cried sharply, "what's the matter?"

Whereupon Katherine ran to his side, clutched him by the arm, and sobbed, "I thought God was dead. For weeks you have been running the universe alone and trying to keep from us the news that God is gone."

We can picture Martin Luther standing there, amazement sweeping over his broad, open face as her thrust of wit went home; then throwing back his head to roar with healing laughter. So he could become again the man whose life and works were an incarnation of the hymn he wrote, the Reformation hymn:

> A mighty fortress is our God,
>   A bulwark never failing;
> Our helper He, amid the flood
>   Of mortal ills prevailing.
>
> . . . .
>
> And though this world, with devils filled,
>   Should threaten to undo us,
> We will not fear, for God hath willed
>   His truth to triumph through us:
> The Prince of Darkness grim—
> We tremble not for him.

God does not give immunity from trouble. He will give strength to meet and master trouble. He does not eliminate peril, hardship, and suffering; he will help us use them for growth in wisdom, courage, righteousness, and love—for everything that makes the man. No matter what, we can depend upon God for what we need the most. In such confidence we live in any present without yielding to craven fear, we can face any future without surrender to despair. We can make a creative use of trouble.

Not least, trust in God yields the gift of inner peace, peace which the world can neither give nor take away.

As the world measures wealth, our Lord died a poor man. He poured everything he had into his cause. At the end there remained only the beautiful cloak, woven in one piece, which his mother had made for him. And for this the soldiers cast dice while he hung on the cross.

But now we know he was rich in treasure beyond compare. For he had peace, deep and wonderful peace at the center of his being. It was not a bogus peace made of blindness to the evil and hurt of the world; nor was it a shameful peace bought by escaping responsibility to lift the burdens of men and storm the citadels of sin. It was peace born of a quiet, yet mighty, trust in God.

So that night, just before the soldiers came to get him, he said to his few remaining friends: "Peace I leave with you, my peace I give unto you: not as the world giveth, give I unto you. Let not your heart be troubled, neither let it be afraid." (K.J.V.)

That was his last will and testament. He bequeathed his friends his peace. It is available to us now—peace, as Marguerite Bro has said, "As sure as sunrise, as indestructible as the winds, as permeating as air, as quiet as starlight, as steady as the hills." [1]

Our line reaches back to the grandeur of those who from the heart could say:

[1] Marguerite Harmon Bro, *Every Day a Prayer* (New York & Chicago: Willett, Clark & Co., 1943), p. 300.

I will lift up my eyes to the hills.
From whence does my help come?
My help comes from the Lord,
    who made heaven and earth.

This is not a blind stab in the dark. This is an interpretation of the universe and of human destiny which stands firmly on the rock of reason. It is validated by experience.

Trust in God. This is the faith of our fathers. This is our heritage. Let us lift up our eyes!

chapter sixteen

DOES CHRIST SAVE US?

"For god so loved the world, that he gave his only begotten Son." If the New Testament had a headline, that would be it.

Then, still in boldface, would follow this: "that whosoever believeth in him should not perish, but have everlasting life. For God sent not his Son into the world to condemn the world; but that the world through him might be saved" (K.J.V.).

That is the gospel in miniature, the ultimate essence of the good news spoken to the world by Jesus Christ.

Do we believe this? If so, why? We call Jesus Christ Savior. What do we mean?

A high-school youth inquires, "How does Christ save us? He lived a long time ago in a faraway place. Our church-school teacher says Jesus is our Savior. The minister preaches about Jesus saving people. What do they mean?"

In the Communion service we read these sacred and solemn words:

"If any man sin, we have an advocate with the Father, Jesus Christ the righteous: and he is the propitiation for our sins: and not for ours only, but also for the sins of the whole world. This is a faithful saying, and worthy of all acceptation, that Christ Jesus came into the world to save sinners."

Then as we hold the bread and later the wine, a minister repeats words of which his lips are not worthy. In an act of remembrance we put ourselves about a table where his first friends had gathered for what would be their last supper with him, and we hear him tell the meaning of his death on the morrow: "This is my body, which is given for you. . . . This cup is the new covenant in my blood, which is shed for you."

How can we believe it? Why is the Cross the supreme symbol for Christians? Why should the execution of an innocent man by Roman soldiers on a cross twenty centuries ago in a faraway place have any relevance for us today, to say nothing of the profoundly personal and social, intimate and imperative significance implied in and by the ritual of Holy Communion?

How does Christ save us? No question probes more deeply. No question reveals more completely the inadequacy of any preacher, especially this preacher. But, though the truth is so big our tiny minds can embrace but a fragment of it; though our speech falters and fails under the burden of telling the little we do know; though it is so vast it sweeps us to the threshold of infinity and there sends us to our knees before grandeur unspeakable, mystery unfathomable, "lost in wonder, love, and praise"—even so, a Christian must give such answer as he can. This he owes the world, himself, and his Savior.

"How does Christ save us?" Let us begin by considering answers given by the early Christians. As they reflected upon what Jesus had said respecting his nature, mission, and death; also, as they thought upon the experience of God and of new life which had come to them through Jesus, they arrived at a profound and startling conviction. They came to believe his death was not a tragic accident; not a maddening, insane quirk of fate; and—this above all —not a pitiful failure. They saw it as the climax of a purpose which had originated in the heart of God and as a choice freely made by his Son. They viewed it as the inevitable culmination of the mighty task to which Jesus Christ had given himself; that is, the reconciliation of sinful men to a holy God. Supremely, they understood it, not as an occasion of defeat, but of ultimate triumph; not of victory by sin and death, but of victory over sin and death.

In their endeavor to interpret this experience and conviction to others they used such symbols and analogies as were available, those indigenous to the common life of their times, especially those suggested by Jewish beliefs and practices. Hence, from traditional temple ceremonies they took the symbol of sacrifice. As the penitent sinner brought a lamb or a bullock to be slain by a priest upon the altar as atonement for his sins, so they said Christ offered himself upon the cross, a sacrifice slain as atonement for the sins of the whole world. From the law courts they took symbols of judgment of death by a holy God. Christ in his death takes this penalty upon himself, thus saving man. Or, to use the other figure, sin is a debt putting us in frightful, inescapable bondage. By giving his life upon the cross, Christ cancelled that debt, fulfilled every legal demand of violated moral law and benign justice, thus setting man free.

These and similar figures of speech we find throughout the New Testament and, where carried over, in hymns and liturgy of the church. They represent earnest and intelligent endeavor to interpret to the world of nineteen and twenty centuries ago the saving significance of Christ's death on the cross.

Are these answers given by our fathers sufficient for us? Are the symbols and analogies they used adequate for our times? In all respect and gratitude for them, this yet needs to be said. Should we use these theories and symbols as a substitute for our own thinking—and/or should we fail to understand their origin and purpose—they become a hindrance rather than a help. They conceal a great and redemptive truth rather than reveal it; make it repulsive rather than appealing; confusing rather than convincing.

Hence, to answer the question, "How does Christ save us?" it is imperative to go beyond theories and symbols of our fathers, venerated though they are, to the primary sources. We must deal firsthand with the same fundamentals of objective fact and personal experience from which they reasoned and spoke. As they used symbols and analogies indigenous to their times, likewise should we.

Turning to such fundamentals, let us ask the question: "How does Christ save us?"

First, with our fathers in the faith we answer, "Christ saves us through his revelation of God."

All creation reveals its creator. In my study is a miniature flowerpot containing a cluster of daintily made artificial pansies. They were fashioned and given to me by a little girl of a church where I was minister. Every time I look at that

151

gift I am reminded of her happy, friendly face, of her sensitive spirit—itself a budding flower—opening to beauty,
love, and faith. The created reveals its creator.

Even so, God is revealed among us. We see something
of him in the far-shining stars, the glittering sea, the everlasting hills; in the nobility of a Schweitzer, the dedicated
life of an unknown church-school teacher, or in the loving
care of a mother for her babe. But of course, God stands
better revealed in his supreme creation, Jesus Christ.

In him we see all of God that human flesh and spirit can
hold. Indeed, in this sense we dare to say Jesus Christ,
though very man, was also very God; that in him "God
was present, God was speaking, God was acting." [1] And,
as God is better revealed by his supreme creation, Jesus
Christ, so he is best revealed by supreme act of his supreme
creation, namely the willingness of Jesus Christ to die on
the cross for mankind. In the love which sent Christ to the
cross we see the love of God for mankind—or, to put it
in stronger language, we see God in human flesh and spirit
suffering and dying for sinful man, for you and me.

It is one thing to think of Jesus Christ merely as a great
prophet, a famous teacher, an illustrious example, an
honored hero, a noble martyr. He was all of that, of course.
But this does not bend our knees before a cross.

It is quite another matter to believe that in Jesus Christ
God entered our common life; shared the worst that can
befall us; loved us to the uttermost even when we deserted,
betrayed, hated, and killed him; and that he did this so we
might find our way from darkness to light, from death to

[1] Harris Franklin Rall, *Religion as Salvation* (Nashville: Abingdon
Press, 1953), pp. 118-32.

life. To look upon the man Jesus Christ on the cross and believe that he was Almighty God as well, that God took the nails for us—that gives the death of Christ significance, saving significance for any man.

Second, with our fathers in the faith we answer, Christ saves us not only as he reveals the nature of God, but also as he reveals the nature of sin.

As Leslie Weatherhead reminds us, "The nature of sin is such that it blinds us to its own nature." And he adds, "The punishment of sin is essentially the deterioration in character—often unconscious—which follows sin, and which sin sets in motion." [2] Sin is first loathed, then condoned, then embraced. Usually, the longer we practice a sin, the less we regard it as sin, the more reasons we find to justify it, even view it as virtue.

The city or government official who accepts bribes, the bank employee who embezzles, the youth who surrenders to lust, the woman who permits her tongue to become a dagger, the man dishonest in business or profane in conversation: in every case what first was loathed, next was condoned, then embraced.

A man who had played big league baseball once told me how he felt when first he violated the teaching of a Christian home and played Sunday baseball. He said, "I had been taught to revere Sunday as a holy day, to regard it as a trust from God for the great things of the soul. In our home it was set aside for quietness, for worship, for books, music,

[2] Leslie D. Weatherhead, *A Plain Man Looks at the Cross* (Nashville: Abingdon Press, 1945), p. 88.

153

and for the happy fellowship of church and home, for all that refines, exalts, instructs, nurtures and redeems the soul.

"When first I went out to warm up for a Sunday game; listened to the chatter and roar of the crowd and the hucksters crying the sale of popcorn, hot dogs, and beer; and saw in no face little or any thought of God, I felt so ashamed and guilty I could hardly handle the ball. But, you know, as weeks passed, the feeling went away. I got so I hardly thought of Sunday as being something special, except that the crowd was bigger and noisier. I got so I didn't feel guilty about it any more." Then he added, thoughtfully, "I guess that is the way it is with most anything."

Whatever our family teaching or our conscience may tell us about commercial sports on Sunday, the fact remains that any violation of the Ten Commandments or of Christian virtue follows the same pattern. Always the more it is practiced the less it is regarded as sin, the more reasons we find to justify it, even view it as virtue. Sin makes us its creature by building walls that make us immune to the probe of conscience and the appeal of repentance.

Only something breaking in upon us, something which shakes us awake and opens our eyes to the sin that has enthralled and possessed us, can bring deliverance. One day a person told me that after years of heavy drinking, he had stopped. "I haven't taken a drink for twenty-one months," he said. I asked, "What prompted you to do this?" He answered quite simply, "I got the DT's."

What the unspeakable anguish of delirium tremens did for that alcoholic, the cross of Jesus Christ does in much larger measure for every sinner, even you and me, anyone who dares look upon it and think!

As nothing known to man, the Cross strips away all glittering tinsel, all excuses of practicality, all blindness of familiarity, every camouflage, and makes us see sin for what it is—our most deceptive, destructive, cruel enemy. The Cross reminds us that every sin to which we are tempted nailed the pure Christ on the cross; and even now crucifies him afresh. We know that always everything good, pure, true, lovely, holy and joyous is crucified by sin. So the Cross is a battering ram that breaks through every barrier to show us our sins as they really are. And what we see is the strongest reason for penitence we can know.

Now come farther to see that since the Cross reveals supremely both the nature of God and the nature of sin, we can say with our fathers, Christ saves as he releases in our life the redemptive power of love.

God's problem was and is the same as that of any parent or teacher. He cannot compel goodness; he can only educe it. He cannot demand love; he can only invite it. He must leave man free to reject or accept, spurn or cherish. The answer God brings to his problem, even you and me, is love. He would awaken our love for him by first loving us. And in the power of that love he would provide us with a weapon mighty enough to break the grip of evil, a dynamic great enough to launch and sustain us in the adventure of goodness.

Methodism's first TV series was called The Way. The first film of the series was based upon the experience of a young minister serving a church in a rough city neighborhood. Though changes were made to conceal identity, many will be interested to know that it was based upon a true incident in the life of Bishop Donald H. Tippett, distinguished leader in American Methodism. During the early years of his ministry he was serving the Church of All Nations in New York, on the Lower East Side. It was a rough neighborhood and the church provided as best it could a seven-day-a-week program, serving many needs of the people there. Especially, the church majored in youth activities. Among other things it had a swimming pool.

About eight o'clock one Saturday night three young hoodlums stopped in, wanting to establish an alibi for their whereabouts. They planned a holdup in upstate New York that night and wished it known they had been in church elsewhere. They went to his office, staged an argument in his presence about what time it was, and got him to verify it. About then the switchboard buzzed in an adjoining office. Since no one was on duty, Tippett slipped out to answer it. The hoodlums, not knowing why he had left the room and finding him at a telephone, thought he was suspicious and was calling the police. Whereupon they set upon him with brass knuckles filed to sharp points, beating him brutally. When they finished he was an unconscious, bloody heap, one eye gouged out. Thinking he was dead and trying to dispose of his body, they doubled him up and jammed him behind a hall radiator. Then they fled.

Some time later, Gertrude Ederle, the channel swimmer, who was there conducting a course in lifesaving, came out of the pool to check on the time. The hall lights were out and as she walked in bare feet down the marble corridor she chanced to step in a pool of warm blood and slipped.

Startled, she screamed. A custodian came and turned on the lights, so he was found.

The lads went upstate according to their plan, staged the holdup, and in the process killed a night watchman. They were apprehended. The one who committed the murder was sent to Sing Sing and later executed.

In the meantime, Bishop Tippett had been in the hospital, hovering between life and death. One eye had been made useless and there was question as to whether the other could be spared. While there, he had several reasons to think of One who once had gone to a cross. Especially, he thought about the power of redemptive love. As soon as he could, he sent a message to the court asking that the other two lads be paroled under his supervision.

He treated them like sons. One failed to respond, but the other made good. He attended college and graduated. Then, later, the bishop helped him attend a medical school. For the lad had said, "I want to become a doctor, an eye surgeon."

Somewhere in America, on the staff of a hospital, is a distinguished surgeon, an eye specialist. I wonder if there is ever a time when he begins an operation that he does not remember a Saturday night on the Lower East Side in New York and a young minister by the name of Tippett.

Of all things in heaven and on earth, what is so mighty for the salvation of man as love! And where is its power so mighty as when sinful man sees it in the face of God, such a God as Jesus Christ reveals from a cross.

"How does Christ save us?" No question probes more deeply. No question reveals more completely the inade-

157

quacy of any preacher or author. But though the truth is so big our little minds can embrace but a fragment of it, and though our speech falters and fails under the burden of telling the small fragment we do know, even so we must answer as best we can.

With our fathers in the faith we can say Jesus Christ saves us as from the cross he shows us the heart of God; on the cross shows us the full worst of evil; and by the cross releases into our poor, frustrated, twisted souls the redeeming, re-creating power of love.

This is enough to save us, even unto the uttermost.